Calvin Coolidge

Eng. on wood by Timothy Cole St. & Del.

*Bookplate engraved on wood by Timothy Cole,
pre-eminent engraver of the early 20th century, J.C.*

In the heart of Vermont's Green Mountains lies the hamlet of Plymouth Notch. CCMF

Return To These Hills

The Vermont Years of

CALVIN COOLIDGE

By *JANE & WILL CURTIS*
and *FRANK LIEBERMAN*

Foreword by *JOHN COOLIDGE*

Introduction by *HOWARD COFFIN*

ILLUSTRATED WITH MANY OLD PHOTOGRAPHS

CURTIS–LIEBERMAN BOOKS, WOODSTOCK, VERMONT

Cover Painting: "The Swearing in of Calvin Coolidge by His Father"
Artist: Arthur I. Keller, 1923
Collection: President Calvin Coolidge State Historic Site, printed by permission.

Copyright © 1985 by Curtis–Lieberman Books.

Reprinted, 1998, as a commemorative edition for the 75th Anniversary of the
Homestead Inaugural of Calvin Coolidge with the support of The Calvin
Coolidge Memorial Foundation and assistance by Cyndy Bittinger, Executive
Director.

Library of Congress Catalog Number 84-73356

Softcover ISBN 0-930985-01-X

Return To These Hills was set in 10 point Meridien,
Printed by Whitman Communications, Inc., Lebanon, N.H.
Design and Typography by Frank Lieberman.

ACKNOWLEDGEMENTS

WE want to thank John and Florence Coolidge for letting us read the diaries of Victoria Josephine Coolidge and the boyhood diaries of her son Calvin. They talked with us about the people of Plymouth Notch and times gone by, as did Ruth Aldrich, Earle Brown, Eliza and Charles Hoskison, Violet and Herman Pelkey, Richard Moore and Clifford Wheeler. Janet Blanchard, Regina Hall and Kenneth Webb, all of Plymouth, generously shared with us their extensive research as did Milton Moore, former Director of the Black River Museum of Ludlow, Vermont. John Dumville of the Vermont Division for Historic Preservation was most helpful in aiding us obtain old photographs. Lawrence Wikander, curator of the Coolidge Collection at the Forbes Library in Northampton, Massachusetts, was another who gave generously of his time.

We especially wish to thank John Lutz, President, and Kathleen Donald, Executive Secretary of the Calvin Coolidge Memorial Foundation of Plymouth, both of whom were of immeasurable help.

The purpose of the Foundation is to assist in protecting and preserving the memorial to President Coolidge which is Plymouth Notch itself. Readers are invited to join the Foundation. Write the Executive Director, Calvin Coolidge Memorial Foundation, Plymouth Notch, Vermont 05056.

We hope that the photographs which illustrate this book will give the reader a real feeling for period and place. For the use of all pictures we are most grateful. Credit for each is given in the captions in the form of small capital letter abbreviations.

BM	Bennington Museum, *Bennington, Vermont*
CCMF	Calvin Coolidge Memorial Foundation, *Plymouth, Vermont*
EB	Earle Brown, *Plymouth Notch, Vermont*
FL	Forbes Library Coolidge Collection, *Northampton, Massachusetts*
JC	John Coolidge, *Plymouth Notch, Vermont*
LOC	Library of Congress, *Washington, D.C.*
VDHP	Vermont Division for Historic Preservation, *Montpelier, Vermont*
VHS	Vermont Historical Society, *Montpelier, Vermont*
WHS	Woodstock Historical Society, *Woodstock, Vermont*

INTRODUCTION

For years I have climbed the hills and mountains of Vermont and one bright summer day several years ago I made my way to a hilltop clearing above Bridgewater and encountered a remarkable view of the Coolidge Range of the Green Mountains and its foothills. Surveying this largely vertical landscape of forested hillsides, the thought occurred that to an unfamiliar observer, there would appear to be no room down in the narrow valleys, the floors of which could not be seen, for a house, let alone a hamlet or village. Yet as a sixth generation Vermonter I full well knew that a remarkable civilization has long flourished there, hemmed in by those steep hillsides. And tiny brooks do flow to rivers, and rivers to larger rivers, and rivers on to the sea. All things are possible. That day the old familiar story of Calvin Coolidge, the legend all Vermont youngsters early on encounter, returned to me. Again I found myself in wonder at the thought that out of one of those little valleys had come a president of the United States. And down there in a house without electricity in a hamlet without street lights, a Vermont farm boy become a man had been given the presidential oath of office by his father in the wee small hours of an early August morning, and had suddenly become the most powerful person in the world.

Just 14 crooked miles east of Plymouth is Woodstock, where I grew up. Woodstock was a town Calvin Coolidge often visited, though he was gone from the earth well before my birth in 1942. Yet any youngster raised near Plymouth in the mid-20th Century had a powerful awareness of Coolidge. As a child, my family could not afford an automobile. Yet my step-grandmother Bertha Metcalf Coffin saw to it, every Sunday afternoon, that one of my uncles made available a car for the Sunday ride. These were educational trips to such places as Fort Ticonderoga, Benson Animal Farm, the White Mountains, the top of Mount Ascutney, the Constitution House in Windsor, and, of course, to Plymouth Notch. I will ever recall Gram Coffin, a truly Victorian woman who dressed in plain clothes, black shoes and wore her hair in a pug, walking about the little village and talking about how Calvin Coolidge grew up there to become "our president." She was fond of quoting from Coolidge's "Bennington" speech, "I love Vermont because of her hills and valleys, her scenery and invigorating climate, but most of all because of her indomitable people." She took particular delight in visiting the Notch cemetery to point out how modest was the presidential headstone, distinguished from others on that historic hillside only by the presidential seal.

It was all fascinating and enjoyable, but in progressing through school, I found that to live in the presence of Coolidge could be daunting. More than one teacher admonished we students that there was no excuse for failure. After all, as Calvin Coolidge had shown us, there was no reason why anyone could not succeed mightily. Coolidge was always with us. My father, Wallace Coffin, was fond of telling how, as a part-time switchboard operator at the Woodstock Telephone Company, he had relayed the call on that historic night in 1923 from Washington to Bridgewater telling the Secret Service to notify Vice President Coolidge that President Harding had died. My mother, Arlene Coffin, who attended commercial college in Northampton, Mass., had worshipped each Sunday at the Church attended by former first lady Grace Coolidge. Mother always said Mrs. Coolidge was "the loveliest lady I ever saw." My grandfather Clarence Coffin, who for more than a half century worked at Gillingham's Store in Woodstock, used to talk of having waited on "President Coolidge." During my summers as the last bell captain at the old Woodstock Inn, I came to know an elderly waitress who served Coolidge there. She said he was always very pleasant, but "didn't tip much." A neighbor, Bill Billings, once told me that his father, a friend of Coolidge's, had confided of "Silent Cal" that once you got him in private, "You couldn't keep him quiet."

Later in life, after going to work for the *Rutland Herald*, I moved to North Shrewsbury and became friends of the remarkable Pierce family. Marjorie Pierce took me one autumn day to the Northam Cemetery to show me the grave of her cousin Aurora Pierce, who had long been housekeeper at the Coolidge home over the ridge at the Notch. That stern and fastidious maiden lady had kept the Coolidge homestead neat as a pin and woe be to the feet not raised when she came through the kitchen when it was time to mop. Also, she saw to it that ALL the contents of the homestead were preserved and when she was carried dying from that house, after nearly 40 years in residence, they finally managed to make out the last words she uttered, over and over. She wanted to be sure that someone locked the door and took the key. Marjorie took me one day to visit another cousin, Ruth Aldrich, known to everyone as "Midge," who lived in the trim white house across the road from the Coolidge birthplace. She operated a tea room during the presidential years and secret servicemen boarded in her tourist cabins. Marjorie and I took tea in her kitchen one gleaming summer day. Midge said to me, "Calvin would come home from Washington, or Northampton, or Boston, and he'd walk around the village. Then he'd come over here to say 'hello' and, why he'd sit right in that chair you're in."

I first met the president's son, John Coolidge, on the United States of America's 200th birthday, July 4, 1976. A church service was held at the

Notch, which I attended with a Ludlow lady, Mary Barton, who worked as a part-time reporter for the *Herald*. Outside the church, in a brilliant mid-summer sunshine, I asked John what Calvin Coolidge would have thought of the country after two centuries. He replied that his father would have been rather pleased generally, though deeply troubled by the growing national debt. Then the presidential offspring turned to my reporter colleague and inquired whether she was the wife of Howard Barton, the man who had come to fix his water pump the previous week. Yes, Mary said, she was. "Well, it hasn't worked right since and I think he ought to get back here and do it right," said Coolidge. I didn't report that aspect of our brief conversation in my *Herald* story that day, but it has struck me down over the years how pure "Coolidge" it was, not to let even the national bicentennial get in the way of dealing with the practical side of life. I must say, the experience confirmed for me reports I'd heard about how John Coolidge could be somewhat aloof and difficult. But as the years passed I visited his home on several occasions, talking with him and his wife Florence, finding them both to be kind, gracious, and full of wonderful stories. My favorite concerns the momentous August 3, 1923, and the morning of the presidential swearing-in. It had been a busy time at Plymouth and the Coolidges employed a local woman, Bessie Pratt, to give Aurora Pierce a hand with household chores. Aurora and Bessie were asleep upstairs in the homestead when word arrived of Harding's death. Of course, well before morning, Colonel Coolidge had administered the Oath of Office to his son down in the parlor, by the light on one of Aurora's spotlessly clean kerosene lamps. But nobody remembered to wake the somewhat deaf housekeeper or her assistant for the great occasion. According to John Coolidge, "Grampa went upstairs to their room and knocked on the door. He apologized for not having got them down to witness the ceremony. Bessie said, "I'll let it go this time, but don't let it happen again."

Through the years I have visited the Notch often, preferring to go there in the late afternoon or evening, when the tourists are gone and all is still. I like to sit on the homestead porch and watch the late New England sunlight fairly blaze on the white clapboard buildings, and see the shadow of the Presidential Range climb East Mountain. As darkness comes down, it is always a quiet thrill to walk about the village knowing I am seeing a scene that has changed so little for generations of Vermonters. I particularly enjoy a stop on the steps of the store, recalling that the president-to-be, as a boy, spent time there in the presence of Civil War veterans gathered evenings around its wood stove. Coolidge went on to develop a deep knowledge of, and a sensitivity to, history.

History visited the Notch on a summer day in 1967, and I was privileged to be there in the company of first lady Lady Bird Johnson where she unveiled, on the Coolidge homestead lawn, the marker designating the Notch a national historic site. Nearly 30 years later, as a trustee of the Calvin Coolidge Memorial Foundation, I was present for her return, and heard her say, "If only more Americans could see the birthplace of their presidents, they would understand them better."

There may be no better way to gain a quick understanding of Plymouth Notch and the extraordinary man it produced than to read the book "Return to These Hills: the Vermont Years of Calvin Coolidge," written by my friends Will and Jane Curtis, of Hartland. These down country New Englanders have written many books since choosing to make Vermont their home, a decision that has earned them a special place in the hearts of our people. First published in 1985, "Return" never received the attention, or the number of printings, it deserved. It did, however, have a considerable moment in the limelight. It was one of two books that the wounded President Reagan read as he recuperated from surgery for his cancer 1985. I discovered the book while working on my own book on Coolidge, and found it to be well written, most informative, entertaining, filled with important photographs, and beautifully designed by the late Frank Lieberman. With the approach of the 75th anniversary of the homestead inaugural, clearly it was time to again bring forth this book.

Only a handful of years ago did I really get to know the Curtises when Will and Jane sought me out and inquired whether I would be willing to cooperate with them on a book about historic sites along the Champlain corridor. We subsequently undertook what proved to be a lengthy and complex project, traveling together the historic waterways from Saratoga, north along the upper Hudson, Lake George, and Lake Champlain, to the stone fortress at Chambly on the Richelieu River. Along the way we discovered many wonderful historic places, and became good friends. It was typical of the zest for life that has allowed them, down the years, to be successful book store operators, farmers, writers, speakers, radio commentators, and much more. When asked to provide an introduction for the reprinted "Return to These Hills," I readily agreed. And so "Return" returns, in 1998, for the three-quarter century celebration of the most fabled presidential inaugural in our great nation's history.

Here among the steep hills and mountains that Coolidge so dearly loved, a remarkable event in the history of the American nation took place. Down at the Notch, where the green hills open just enough to accommodate a tiny village, the hand of history touched down and created a place of wonder. And that place just happened to be one of the most beautiful in all of Vermont, thus making it one of the loveliest on all the Earth. To look down toward it from a high hilltop is to stand amazed that such an event occurred in a far-away little hill valley so narrow the bottom of it cannot be seen. But the event lives and gleams down the long years more bright, certainly, than 10,000 of the kerosene flames that lit the scene in the dark of that fabled August 3 three-quarters of a century ago. As we come to give that events its proper due here on the verge of a new century and millennium, the republication of the Curtises little book strikes me as a way of honoring Calvin Coolidge, his people and his state, that is, in the words of another president who came out of a rural landscape, "altogether fitting and proper."

HOWARD COFFIN

FOREWORD

Plymouth, the birthplace of my father, was always home to him. If it is true that "home is where the heart is," my father's heart was there even when he was far away. He returned to Plymouth as often as he could, and regretted the times when he could not.

Although he saw a great deal of our country during the years he was absent from Plymouth, he said in his 1928 Bennington speech, "...I could not look upon the peaks of Ascutney, Killington, Mansfield and Equinox without being moved in a way that no other scene could move me...".

Letters which my father wrote to his father shortly before his graduation from Amherst indicated clearly his reluctance to leave Plymouth for a life elsewhere. In his autobiography he states that when he finally left home for the purpose of entering the law, the parting was very hard for his father to bear. I suspect the same was true for my father.

Early in his law practice, matters on which he was engaged were so numerous that for three years he did not take the time to visit Plymouth, which I am sure he deeply regretted.

The summer following my birth, my father took my mother and me to Plymouth. I was not quite a year old, and mother was unhappy to have me to care for at that age with the very limited facilities my grandfather's house afforded.

The only running water was that which came from a spring into the cast iron kitchen sink. Hot water was heated in a reservoir in the wood stove, and a tin wash-tub was used for bathing. The toilet was the old fashioned privy. However, undoubtedly my father was happy to be home, and glad to have the chance to show me to my grandfather, whose first name had been given to me.

All through my father's political life he returned to Plymouth whenever he could. He saw to it that my brother and I spent our summer vacations from school there, helping with the work on the farm.

After leaving Washington on March 4, 1929, my father and mother spent their summers in Plymouth. In the summer of 1932, he built an addition to my grandfather's house. This provided room for his books and more modern plumbing facilities.

This addition had no central heating, only fireplaces. However, he and my mother would stay into the fall until the cold weather sent them back to Northampton. He was loathe to leave Plymouth, saying he felt safer there than anywhere.

Unfortunately he did not live long enough to enjoy the new addition except for the first summer. He died the following January. Now he rests in the Plymouth Notch Cemetery with four other generations of forebearers.

JOHN COOLIDGE
Plymouth, Vermont

The road into Plymouth, little different then and now. CCMF

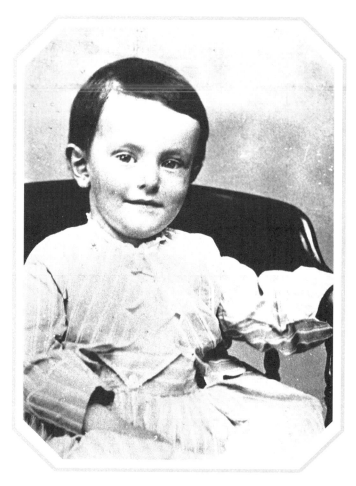

Calvin Coolidge, aged three years. CCMF

I

ROOTS OF THE PAST

ONLY one President of the United States has ever been born on that most American of days, the Fourth of July. That man was Calvin Coolidge, born on that day in 1872 in the remote village of Plymouth Notch, Vermont.

The tale of the small red-headed boy who grew up in a tiny Vermont hamlet and who became the President of the United States, is one that has captured the imagination of the American people.

When Calvin Coolidge was born the town of Plymouth was a quiet backwater and a town without a well defined center. Instead it consisted of a number of hamlets with such picturesque names as the Kingdom and Frog City as well as the Union, the Notch, Tyson, the Five Corners, Ninevah and Dublin. This last was where the Irish laborers hired by iron master Isaac Tyson lived in a small enclave in the midst of Yankeedom.

Today, in winter, the short chill days cast a mantel of silence over the Notch, but in summer the small place swarms with the curious who marvel at the simplicity of the surroundings. There's the country store and the post office with its plain attached ell, the President's birthplace; the spare white church; his father's modest house where the President was brought up and which became a summer White House. The Coolidge cheese factory is up the road apiece; beyond is the one room school. There are four houses, some large barns and the gray Coolidge farm up the lane, the sum total of the little world in which Calvin Coolidge spent his boyhood and to which he returned whenever he could. At the end of the 20th century, when one walks about Plymouth Notch, it's as if one were looking at the artifacts of another age. How, people ask, could the most powerful man in the world return to such a spartan setting? Accustomed to the imperial splendor of succeeding pres-

On the sturdy Glenwood range were cooked all the Coolidge meals, winter and summer. The linen dish towels were woven by Aunt Mede. CCMF

idents, the visitor stares in surprise at the homey worn quality of the sitting room and the simple furniture of the parlor; at the kitchen sink where the President of the United States washed his hands before sitting down to eat at the kitchen table.

It seems clear that he felt the need to come back to his roots, to refresh himself with the sight of mountains and small rushing brooks. The undemanding friendliness of the people he grew up with must have helped to shield him for a spell from the unrelenting glare of publicity that accompanied his every move while in office and in turn the villagers regarded him as a friendly, warm hearted man, a good neighbor.

The Plymouth Notch we see today is little changed from that of Calvin Coolidge's boyhood. Earle Brown, who remembers the Plymouth of President Coolidge, says the greatest changes are the everyday sounds. No longer does one hear the ring of the axe as next year's fuel supply is cut in the woodlot. Gone are the squeals of the iron-shod runners of a sleigh as it slides over snow and the cheerful sleigh bells' jingle. Who listens now for the mellow tone of the cow bell on old Daisy as she led her companions down to the pasture gate at evening milking? Or who could today recognize the melancholy hooting on the further hill as that of a lovesick bear?

But even the first Vermont Coolidge, Captain John, would have recognized the fertile, rolling meadows set like a green bowl among the hills. By the time John Coolidge of Bolton, Massachusetts, arrived in Vermont about 1780, much of the valley land had been already settled. It was just after the French and Indian Wars had ended in 1760 that settlers from the older colonies commenced pouring into what was then the American frontier in search of cheap land. Within a decade these early townships in the Champlain and Connecticut valleys, first settled in 1761, became centers for trade and water-powered industries. They evolved into towns adorned with handsome dwellings, substantial public buildings, populated by well-educated influential citizens. After the Revolution came another influx of settlers, soldiers with money in their pockets.

The Coolidge family tradition has it that John Coolidge, who had fought at Lexington and Bunker Hill, first saw Plymouth when he marched with his regiment through Vermont to Fort Ticonderoga. His way led along General Amherst's old Crown Point Road, and when the

Plymouth's last log cabin, still standing in the 20s. Captain John's first dwelling probably resembled this one. VDHP

A landscape such as this persuaded John Coolidge to settle in Plymouth.

young captain saw the beautiful Black River Valley and the mountain lakes nestled in the hills he decided he'd best use his pay to buy land. Who knew what might happen to the coin of the new country?

About 1780 he returned and took up a claim and built a house whose cellar hole is still discernible today. Although Salt Ash, as Plymouth township was then called, had been granted a charter in 1761, no-one had ventured that way until one John Mudge cleared a farm two years before Captain John arrived on the scene. Up in the isolated hills the catamount, bear and wolf still roamed, undisturbed by the few humans. The land was high, almost 1400 feet about sea level but there was space aplenty, and at that time all land, high or low, was deemed cultivatable.

So the young Massachusetts soldier took up land in what was for many years the most isolated town in Vermont, survived the first cruelly hard years along with his courageous wife and was able to pass on to his descendants, son Calvin, grandson Calvin Galusha, great-grandson John and great-great-grandson John Calvin, his hardwon pioneering skills and his land.

But the frontier excitement and hope of the early years began to wane as the settlers discovered that the first wonderful yields were due to unused soils which were soon exhausted. The weather, winters lasting from late October to late April, discouraged many, especially the infamous year of 1816 when snow fell every month of the year. "Eighteen Sixteen and Froze to Death," Vermonters called it. News of fertile, easily-worked soils to the west began to drift up to the hill farms and little by little the restless and ambitious commenced to move away. The 1830s were the last in which Vermont held to its population gains; after that, and particularly after the Civil War, there was a wholesale abandonment of the hill farms. Leaving their hard won fields to grow to brush or selling to prosperous sheep farmers, abandoning their houses to tumble into cellerholes, the hill farmers moved to the new lands of Illinois or Wisconsin. Only the lilac bushes that had been carefully brought from down country by settlers' wives remained to bloom beside the forgotten doorsteps.

Not all were happy with their move. Some, appalled by the endless prairies, were anxious to return to Vermont's comfortable, narrow valleys. Other unfortunates, feeling their last hour upon them, pleaded that their bodies be shipped home. Twenty-four year old Barton Billings, Galusha Coolidge's nephew, dying in Quindaro, Kansas, requested that his friends, "Carry me back to old Vermont, where the rills trickle down the hills, that is where I want to go when I die." Not only was his request honored but his last words were engraved on his tombstone in the Notch cemetery.

Plymouth was touched by the exodus from the hill country. Those who stayed behind saw with sorrow the empty houses about them. A hundred and fifteen of their friends and relations left during the twenty years between 1850 and 1870. In addition, the bright prospects of prosperity to be gained from Plymouth's mineral resources had also vanished. The iron ore deposits that Isaac Tyson had mined and from which he made stoves at this foundry, were depleted. A small amount of soapstone and marble had been extracted and the gold boom had come and gone. Returning "Forty-niner" Hankinson had claimed to have seen "color" in Plymouth's hills and indeed some nuggets were found but no great amount. The only persons who actually made money from Plymouth's gold mines were a shady bunch of out-of-towners who bought the mines, salted them with gold nuggets, sold shares to the unwary and departed in the middle of the night. The only mineral that prospered its owners was limestone, which, when heated in kilns, made especially good plaster, much in demand by those building fine houses in such wealthy towns as nearby Woodstock.

The great railway boom of the '40s had come and gone; leaving Plymouth stranded in the mountains. The nearest station was twelve miles away in Ludlow, the chief marketing town in the area and where prosperous woolen mills were situated. Plymouth Notch folk were not entirely cut off from the outside world, however, for a stage ran through the village twice daily on a round trip from Bridgewater to Ludlow. The one way fare was seventy-five cents, not cheap considering wage rates. But those who lived at the Five Corners, half a mile southeast of Plymouth Notch, fared worse; in their mountain fastness they were liable to be completely isolated in the dead of winter. The Five Corners, once the most populous village in the township, boasting a hotel as late as 1900, has vanished completely, leaving only five woodroads leading to a little clearing in the forest.

A woods road near Plymouth.

Captain John had left five farms to his five children, his son Calvin inheriting the one at the Notch. Calvin prospered, but his house burned to the ground not long after it was built. He then built the substantial four-square Coolidge farm house with its imposing barn, still standing today. The Notch was a quiet place; outsiders had little reason to venture up the winding roads that led to it. There was a store, a school, a blacksmith shop, a church without a minister and six or seven farms. Most of the inhabitants were Vermonters born and bred, lean, rugged and self-reliant. Their lives were concerned with the endless tasks that have kept countrymen busy year 'round from time immemorial as season followed season. The labor unrest that erupted after the Civil War, the flood of foreign workers who flocked to cities, the periodic booms and busts, scarcely touched them.

But if they were spared the troubles of the bigger towns and cities, they also missed much of the intellectual stimulus of the American Renaissance of the time, the world of Dr. Oliver Holmes, Henry Thoreau and Harriet Beecher Stowe. As Claude Fuess said in his biography, *Calvin Coolidge, The Man From Vermont*, "President Coolidge came from the New England of Ethan Frome, not that of Emerson."

Although the Coolidges were of the Puritan stock that first settled New England, they had no place in the "codfish aristocracy" which flourished in the northern seacoast cities. Distantly related to the Coolidges of Boston, they had been content to lead lives of hardworking upcountry folk in contrast to the distinguished careers of the Boston branch. That is, until the Vermont family produced a President of the United States.

But if in many ways the life in Plymouth Notch was that of a quiet backwater, it was also one of great rewards, soul satisfying if seldom financially enriching. To a farmer there is no greater contentment than to see his barn well filled with cattle and hay, to his wife to know that the

This large house belonged to neighboring farmer James S. Brown. VDHP

Hiram D. Moor and wife Abigail. FL

Below, their three daughters. Victoria Josephine is at the right with her sisters Mary and Sarah. VDHP

Opposite, the house where John Coolidge lived as a boy. VDHP

larder shelves are crammed with a winter's supply of food for the family. The barns of the Coolidges were large and capacious, the mark of successful farmers, their homes spacious and comfortable. Although they may not have voiced their love for their hills, they knew no more beautiful landscape existed anywhere. "No Coolidge ever went west," it is said. They didn't want to; they were doing very well where they were.

Grandfather and Grandmother Moor lived in the big house in the center of Plymouth Notch. It had once been a tavern serving the travellers on the road between Bridgewater and Ludlow and had boasted a bar-room and an upstairs dance hall. Grandfather Moor, upon moving in, had at once removed these sites of dubious pleasure.

Just up the lane was the Coolidge farm where Calvin Galusha and his wife Sarah Almeda lived with their sons John Calvin and Julius Caesar. He loved the life of farming so dearly that he hoped to tie his only grandson to the land by deeding to the boy a part of the farm, the Lime Kiln Lot.

Tall and handsome, Calvin Galusha's vitality is evident in his pictures. A glint of a smile hovers about his face, perhaps thinking of the practical jokes he was so partial to, a fondness inherited by his grandson. In the midst of hardworking pragmatic folk, "Galoosh" as he was called, found time to keep such useless but beautiful creatures as peacocks and other gaily colored fowl and carefully tended a garden full of scarlet flowers. He loved to see puppies and colts gamboling about and was known as an expert horseman and breeder of Arabian horses. Perhaps his love of young

Calvin Galusha Coolidge. FL   *Sarah Almeda Brewer Coolidge.* FL

and beautiful animals kept him from pursuing the universal masculine sports of hunting and fishing.

An able and popular man (except with those on whom he practiced his jokes), he held many public offices from constable to Representative in the Vermont General Assembly. Young Calvin at an early age was imbued with the idea that responsible men did their part in serving the public.

Calvin was close to his Grandfather Coolidge, the older man calling him "My Cal"; perhaps in Galusha's heart Calvin was filling the void left by the death of his second son, Julius Caesar Coolidge, more than two years before Calvin's birth. The older man not only taught him to ride and to ride standing on a horse's back but took time to point out to his grandson the beauties of the hills and streams and meadows about him, lessons the boy never forgot. While Calvin Galusha lay dying, confined to his bed, he often asked that Calvin come in and read the Bible to him, for companionship during the long days and to gain comfort from the words. Calvin was glad to be of help to his Grandfather although the six year old boy had a hard time struggling with some of the longer words. There was a strong streak of sentiment in Calvin Coolidge; it meant a great deal to him to know that Grandfather had read the same passages to his grand-father, Captain John. He carefully kept his grandfather's Bible, placing his hand upon it when taking the oath as President from his father.

Grandmother Coolidge, tall handsome Sarah Almeda Brewer, possessed a character to match that of her energetic husband. Sarah's thick dark hair, severely parted in the middle, remained black all her long life. With no regular minister at the Plymouth Notch Church, it was she who provided a religious service in the community, keeping a Sunday School until she was an old lady. Although President Coolidge joined a church only after becoming President, his strong sense of moral rightness and deep faith in God reflected his grandmother's strict upbringing. "I stayed with her at the farm much of the time and she had much to do with shaping the thought of my early years." As a Baptist she disapproved of dancing, and it is said that she once promised to give Calvin a dollar if he stayed away from a village dance. The value of a dollar appealed to the boy, and he didn't go. "The Coolidges never dance," Plymouth folk said but Calvin, at worldly Amherst College, did try a few lessons. Alas, they didn't take, much to his lively future wife's regret.

For all her strict Calvinistic beliefs, "Aunt Mede," as everyone called her, provided a safe haven for Calvin after his mother died. "Aunt Mede's heart was a big one with room for everyone," said her grandson. As a young mother she and Galusha took in his sister's two children, brought them up as their own and when her daughter-in-law Victoria died, she mothered the two grandchildren. She encouraged Calvin's intellectual bent by lending him books from her library and in the winter evenings read aloud from exciting books, *The Rangers*, or *The Tory's Daughter* and the *Green Mountain Boys of Vermont*.

She must have provided not only a warm familiar place for her grandchildren but one that satisfied the eye as well, for she loved fine china, some of which is still treasured by her descendants. She faithfully kept the barn yard filled with Galusha's exotic fowl and maintained his beloved scarlet flower garden. Strict as she could be, she indulged her only grandson. One of the reasons, he told his friends, he liked to spend so much time at her house was because she let him sleep with his socks on. In fact, he spent so much time at the farm his father John said dryly that Calvin had a "cast iron arrangement" with her.

John, Galusha Coolidge's older son, much to his father's displeasure, had given up farming to become a storekeeper. (He had also taught for a term down at the Pinney Hollow school.) Down the lane lived a beautiful young lady who bore the name of two empresses, Victoria Josephine. She had been brought up in the large house now known as the Wilder House in the center of the village, daughter of prosperous Abigail and Hiram Moor. She had lacked for nothing, was sent away for a year to the Black River Academy in Ludlow with its courses in English literature and had been given on her twenty-second birthday, $60.00, a tidy sum in 1868.

Victoria Josephine Moor. FL   *John Calvin Coolidge.* VDHP

She fell in love with the tall taciturn young man on the farm next door. In the course of things she would have moved into the large comfortable Coolidge farmhouse. Instead she found herself destined to set up housekeeping in the cramped quarters behind the village store.

Victoria's courtship was a stormy one; her fiancé, his mind on his impending break from the family and his new business, was often neglectful of her. "Business before pleasure" John would say to her when she complained that he had not been on hand to escort her home from a village social. Just before opening date she volunteered to help clean up the store but, "for all the thanks I got you could put it in your eye." She had doubts about the marriage, "I am a fool as near as I can make out…" But in the end Victoria and John were married in the parlor of her father's house. She wore a "whoop" skirt under a stylish gray silk dress she had made herself and drove off on her honeymoon in Woodstock through the soft May evening.

Next Sunday John and Victoria dutifully appeared in Church. The bemused congregation agreed that never had such a handsome couple been seen in their midst.

On the morning of July 4th, 1872, John left his bird's-eye maple and cherry counters and opened the door in the back of the store that led to the family quarters. There his young wife lay in the tiny downstairs bedroom.

John Coolidge's store. In the rear is the unpainted ell where his son was born. Below; the birthplace (open door) from the rear. VDHP

There is a report that Calvin Galusha Coolidge sent his hired man to fetch the doctor five miles away. Whether or not he got there in time is not recorded but nearby Mrs. Polly Brown was summoned by the baby's other grandfather. "Victoria is going to have a little tea party and wants you to come." A little girl listening wondered why anyone would have a tea party in the middle of the morning. The baby's paternal grandmother was there too, capable Sarah Almeda Brewer Coolidge. During her long lifetime she assisted at the birth of over a hundred babies and must have brought cheerful reassurance in the days when doctors travelled over miles of difficult roads in their buggies.

The little girl, Avis Brown, remembered years later that her mother came back from the morning tea party saying, "Victoria's got a little boy." The little boy, John Calvin Coolidge (he later dropped the "John"), was born into a closeknit family, whose members lived respectable lives, helping their community in many ways, leaders in a quiet society.

As with any newborn grandson he was cosseted and loved, his baby ailments worried over, for babyhood and young childhood were dangerous years in the 19th century when such fearsome epidemics as diphtheria and scarlet fever swept the country. Luckily, young Calvin, according to his father, was spared such ordeals but the Plymouth Notch Cemetery is filled with pitiful reminders that most families were not so fortunate. The Bradley family, neighbors of the Coolidges, had seven children. One died at birth; then within days four, three girls and a little boy, were swept away in an epidemic and the next year their remaining son died. Only Elsie, the youngest, survived to grow up to be a school teacher.

Abigail Grace Coolidge, aged four. CCMF

When Calvin was almost three, sister Abigail Grace was born, a plump cheerful child. In a tightly knit family of parents and two sets of grandparents, the brother and sister, both intelligent young people, established a close bond of understanding and companionship, one that endured until Abbie died tragically at the age of fourteen.

Although Victoria's schooling had been ended after a year at Black River Academy, she had an innate love of poetry and awareness of the beauty of the world about her. She loved to watch sunsets throwing the western hills into relief, to look out the window to see the winter stars entangled in the maples' bare branches. Her son said, "It seemed as though the rich green tints of the foliage and the blossoms of the flowers came for her in the springtime, and in the autumn it was for her that the mountainsides were struck with crimson and gold." In her last years he remembered how she would sit with him in the open doorway trying to get her breath in the sweet autumn air and to catch a final glimpse of the October sun. She was a consumptive, a victim of that dread killer of the late 19th century, and became soon after her marriage, a chronic invalid. "But, she used what strength she had in lavish care upon me and my sister…"

From her Calvin Coolidge inherited his slight frame, delicate features, his reddish hair and light complexion. From her, too, he got the sensitive nature which he took great pains to hide from the world, and, unfortunately, his tendency to illness. All his life he kept the memory of her tender love close to his heart and always had her picture on his desk and another one in a silver locket that he kept on his person. By the age of twelve, when he suffered the terrible blow of her death, much of her character was stamped upon him. The morning after the midnight inauguration, on his way to Washington he had the limousine stop at the cemetery so that he might stand at his mother's grave for a few moments.

The last winter of his mother's life Calvin and sister Abbie spent as much time as they could by their mother's side as she lay on the couch in the sitting room. There she could be in the center of the family doings and talk to Martha McWain as she went about her work in the kitchen. For the children, it was as if they were trying to store up memories against the time when she would be gone. She lived through a bitter January. It was almost sugaring time when one night his father came to Calvin's bedroom and told him to come down to bid farewell to his mother. "…we knelt down to receive her final blessing. In an hour she was gone. It was her thirty-ninth birthday. I was twelve years old. We laid her away in the blustering snows of March. The greatest grief that can come to a boy came to me. Life was never to seem the same again." In the months that followed, neighbors could often see the lonely boy walking slowly in the dusk down to the village cemetery.

Carrie Brown in her graduation dress. FL.

For six years John Coolidge tried to be mother and father to his motherless children. Then he made one of the happiest decisions of his life. He proposed to Miss Carrie Brown whose family lived in Plymouth Notch as long as had the Coolidges.

She was a fine substitute for Victoria Josephine, loving books, music and children. She had been an exceptionally intelligent little girl. A young teacher who went on to head New Hampshire's Normal schools said that she was the brightest pupil he had in fifty years of teaching. Carrie graduated from Kimball Union Academy across the river in New Hampshire, and became a teacher herself, the only profession then open to bright young women.

John Coolidge built the two story bay window for his new wife, making a sunny spot for her plants and upstairs she placed her sewing machine so she could see the store. When the stage came in sight she would hurriedly throw a shawl across her shoulders and run across the road to take up her duties as village postmistress. Her house was the after-school-hours-center for children, fresh cookies and milk waiting in the warm kitchen, her new piano in the parlor to listen to, the porch and yard to play in. Her only restriction was that they were not to swing on the little cedar tree in front of the house, one that she treasured. The little sapling has grown into a fine stout patriarch, but its divided trunk does tell that some young people used it more vigorously than Mrs. Coolidge liked.

In a village that provided its own entertainment, Carrie Coolidge could be counted on to coach the children for their parts in plays given in the hall over the store. Colonel John would sit by quietly, not saying anything but not missing anything either.

"Carrie Brown was a Coolidge lady, all the Coolidge wives are ladies you know," says Mrs. Charles Hoskison of Plymouth who treasures the memories of the warm, loving woman who opened her heart to children of all sorts.

Long-time Plymouth resident Clifford Wheeler remembers that she never forgot to send down to the Wheeler house on the Bridgewater road

John Coolidge added the two-story bay window for Carrie Brown. CCMF

a bag of oranges and a big box of ribbon candy; very welcome at Christmas time with nine children in the family.

Ernest Carpenter in his *Boyhood Days of President Calvin Coolidge* tells a story of Amos Butler and his trained heifer and Carrie Brown. Amos was a backward boy, much ridiculed by other children, who possessed nothing of his own but a heifer which he had trained to drive like a horse. One day Ernest Carpenter saw Amos draw up in his carriage to a group of villagers who thought to have a bit of fun with him. "Let's have a picture of you Amos, and how about one of the ladies climbing in with you." Amos was pleased at the idea but not the ladies, each one declining until the young teacher, Carrier Brown, came by and grasped the situation. "If all you women are afraid I am not." Tucking her skirts about her she climbed in beside Amos Butler and was duly photographed. A faded old picture shows Amos in a large straw hat, bending over his reins while Carrie sits straight upright, holding an umbrella over her head as proud as if the carriage was drawn by Queen Victoria's horse instead of a little red and white cow. Her stepson said of her, "For thirty years she watched over me and loved me, welcoming me when I went home, writing me often when I was away, and encouraging me in all my efforts. When at last she sank to rest she had seen me made Governor of Massachusetts and knew I was being considered for the Presidency."

Carrie Brown with Amos Butler in his heifer-drawn buggy.

John Calvin Coolidge. FL

The prime influence in young Calvin's life was his father. He speaks of him more often than any other person in his autobiography and with the greatest admiration. Because he was with his father a great deal after Victoria died, he was able to see him act in a number of difficult roles. It seemed to the boy that there was nothing his father could not do. Besides being a shrewd businessman, John Coolidge was an accomplished carpenter, brick and stone mason and buggy maker. The best buggy he ever owned was the one he made when as a young man he was an apprentice to a carriage maker. It has to be understood that in the country the only professional artisan was the smith without whose expert knowledge in making and repairing tools and machinery, the countryside would not function. The skills of John Coolidge were those needed by any successful farmer, for it was a do-it-yourself age. John Coolidge simply did these tasks more efficiently than many of his neighbors. Household waterpipes and tinware were a matter of course repaired at home, for plumbers resided only in large towns. A sick animal could not survive long enough for a veterinarian to arrive over miles of rutted roads, a cure must be effected by the owner. John Coolidge was trained by his animal-loving father and performed many delicate operations on the animals under his care. Minor repairs on a damaged rod on a mowing machine he had to make, for it might take months before a part could be sent from the factory.

Young Calvin was proud of his able efficient father and saw, too, how careful he was with his money. Prudent thriftiness was a watch word in the Coolidge household and indeed a quality most admired in the hill

The village store was the place to meet. John Wilder, left, and his brother-in-law John Coolidge make themselves comfortable beside the stove. CCMF

country. "Use it up, wear it out, make it do or do without," was a favorite motto. John Coolidge was careful with his money, but he knew how to make it, too. In the limited economy of Plymouth Notch, he was a successful businessman. He rented the old store building for $40 a year and in a year's time had made a profit of $1,200. In 1876 he had prospered enough to feel able to buy the house across the road from the store for $375 and made money on that by selling a barn on the place. At his death in 1926 he left a tidy estate of $70,000.

The new house into which he moved his family was a visible sign of success. Black walnut furniture from Boston graced the parlor and later a piazza was added, an almost unheard-of luxury in the hill country. It was evident to young Calvin from watching his father that by industrious hard work and prudence in spending money earned, one could prosper, a theme often heard in Coolidge's speeches.

John decided after inheriting his father's property to sell the store to his brother-in-law, Franklin Moor, and to live on the proceeds from his father's land.

Retirement from the store left him with time for public service. He filled almost every office available. He served as selectman, tax collector, road commissioner, constable, deputy sheriff and school commissioner. He was also school superintendent and in 1884 received $11.40 for his efforts. He served in the Vermont General Assembly as Representative and as Senator and to top off his public career was given the honorary title of "Colonel" while on Governor Stickney's staff. He much relished the destinction and enjoyed having folk refer to him as "Colonel John." Because he had a good working knowledge of the law and because there were no lawyers in Plymouth he was often asked to draw up wills and to deputize for the attorneys in Ludlow and Woodstock. As deputy sheriff Colonel John had a unique method of dealing with the accused criminals he was charged with in the prisonless village of Plymouth Notch. He would escort the accused to the Coolidge house, feed him and then bed him down in the "shed bedroom" after carefully removing every article of clothing. Next morning, fully clothed, the prisoner would be taken to the county jail in Woodstock. Often he would take his young son along to the court and Calvin saw how his father dealt diplomatically with potentially tricky situations. As an important figure in town, John Coolidge, acting as selectman or school superintendent, was an example of the role responsible men must play in society, large or small.

Calvin was proud that although Plymouth Notch was a tiny community, his father through his public service, was known far outside the town, from the most humble bank teller in Ludlow (John Coolidge was vice-president of the bank) to the Governor of the State.

Today, the Coolidge Homestead looks much as it did in Calvin's youth. VHS

II

A COUNTRY BOY

As the young boy stepped out into the world beyond the kitchen, he tumbled about in the yard with the family pets, learning that teased cats scratch and hungry dogs bite when interrupted at eating. Grandfather Galusha's farm was a fascinating place. Something was always happening there. In the winter the barn was a haven of peace and quiet, especially when a storm was blustering outside. It was full of quiet sounds; the soft swish of milk into a pail at milking time (what fun it was to see the barn cat stand on its hind legs when the hired man directed a stream of milk into its open mouth!) The wooden stanchions creaked as the cows searched for a wisp of hay in the feed trough, a new calf might bleat and a heavy hoof thump as one of the horses shifted its weight. He learned just where a cow likes to be scratched behind its horns and that you must always hold your palm flat when offering horses a bit of carrot. The barn smelled of good things, hay, fresh milk, clean animals.

The cows were beautiful, too, white with huge black patches and the softest eyes imaginable.

Out in Grandmother's hen house it was like a treasure hunt to collect the day's eggs in a basket, being careful not to upset the cross old rooster who could give a boy's bare legs a good hard nip. But Grandfather's collection of strange birds! Some had feathery legs with black tails and there were little ones that tried to pick fights with the big roosters and there were the peacocks, why they must be the most beautiful birds in the world. Calvin would never let a feather be thrown away. He felt proud to call this man "Grandfather;" who else had peacocks sweeping their wonderful tails around their farm? And who else tended a flower garden with such brilliant flowers in it? Most men wouldn't put their nose inside a flower garden but Grandfather Coolidge had a garden where he grew the

Farm wives raised the poultry but it was the children's task to collect the eggs. In the fall the chickens and turkeys were prepared for the city markets. This was almost the only way for country women to earn a little pin money. VHS

To the right is a poster advertising Calvin Galusha's prize Arabian stallion for stud. Arabian horses were the Rolls Royces of the animal world. EB

brightest, reddest flowers he could find, cannas and dahlias big as baseballs and orange nasturtiums.

Grandfather knew and loved good horseflesh too. In the days before the automobile, nothing could give a countryman more pride than to own a fine horse of his own breeding, gentled and trained by himself. Grandfather had a reputation as a breeder of fine Arabians, aristocrats of the horse world. There was nothing more pleasurable to do in the evening than to stand by the gate to the horse pasture when chores and supper were done with and to watch a new colt frisk about in the cool air. It was Calvin Galusha who first set his young grandson on the back of a horse at the age of three and then taught him to stand up. As might have been expected there was a tumble and Calvin fell off breaking an arm. Broken arms and legs weren't feared like sicknesses and he was soon back by his grandfather's side. Horseback riding was one of the two sports he enjoyed in later years, but even that wasn't an unalloyed pleasure. Horse dander bothered his asthma so he had a mechanical horse installed in the White House basement, causing not a few snickers at the thought of the President jogging solemnly up and down in the cellar. But in his youth he could wander off by himself on his calico horse as no one else cared to ride. "But a horse is much company, and riding over the fields and along the country roads by himself, where nothing interrupts his seeing and thinking, is good occupation for a boy. The silences of Nature have a discipline all their own."

Riding on top of the world! VHS

Vice-President Coolidge never forgot how to pitch hay. FL

In summer time the little boy would be hoisted on the flat bed of the hay wagon as it trundled out along the lane to the hay fields where the sweet grass had been cured and gathered together in haycocks. He must stay out from under the wagon for the oxen might start up unexpectedly, moving from cock to cock. And be especially careful not to get in the way of the men as they speared great forks full of hay and pitched them up on the wagon. The best fun of all was to scramble up with the help of a good-natured boost to the top of the load. A boy could hardly look out over a wall of hay on either side but up there he was king of the world!

Lots of wood was needed for cooking and heating. VHS
Below; a one horse-power treadmill made wood cutting easy. VHS

In summer, too, was the delightful task of going with mother or the hired girl to take switchel to the hayers. The children could watch the preparation of the drink, cold water and vinegar with molasses to sweeten and a good shaking of ground ginger, then taste it to see if it was sweet enough. Then it was poured into a wooden switchel jug and carried out to the hayfield. The men who had been going around the edge of the field with scythes would stop, wipe off their foreheads and then

their blades and give them a few swipes of the sharpening stone before sitting in the shade of the stone wall. How cool and how sweet and yet tart the switchel tasted on a hot day!

Country children learned that hard work was a part of life, the most important part it often seemed. Older children must keep an eye on the baby and four year old Calvin was doubtless entrusted to mind little Abigail. Toys were scarce in the Notch and he must learn to share with his sister. At five he was too young to help very much around the house but it wasn't too early to see that the woodbox was kept full, summer and winter. No matter how hot the day might be, the kitchen range had to be kept going in order to cook the hearty three-times-a-day meals expected by all men. It was an endless chore to see that there was plenty of kindling available to the housewife and that when she reached for a stick in the woodbox it was at hand. Keeping the box filled was a boy's work; it was a serious breach of the family's trust if he fell down on the job. Once young Calvin remembered in the middle of the night that he hadn't replenished the box after supper. He quietly got dressed and crept downstairs to the woodshed. When someone asked sleepily what he was up to, "Filling the woodbox," was the answer. No one thought it odd to do it at midnight, they knew that the box had to be full before breakfast.

Calvin's mother wasn't strong enough to do the housework all by herself. Her husband, hoping to spare her, hired a young girl, Martha McWain, a Coolidge cousin, to help keep the house tidy. This was not unusual, busy housewives with large households to cook for and gardens and fowl to tend, often had a neighbor's daughter to come and live in. The girls didn't think of themselves as going to work as a servant, there was no loss of social position, they were simply "helping out." They shared the life of the family as if it were their own. Indeed some young women were literally adopted and spent their whole life with their surrogate family. Aurora Pierce, who came to help out Carrier Brown Coolidge, and who became Colonel John's housekeeper, spent a total of forty years under the Coolidge roof, and ruled every member with an iron hand.

Calvin Coolidge remembered as a youngster having to stay at home if the only place in the buggy was wanted by the hired girl or boy. Born in him was the democratic spirit of the Vermont small town, a spirit which stood him in good stead in his political career. All his life Calvin Coolidge possessed a refreshing lack of social pretensions and was endowed with a curiosity about people's lives and had a way of conveying his interest that was flattering, not prying. One of the first letters he wrote on returning to Washington as President was to his old shoemaker friend in Northampton, Mr. Lucey. "...I want you to know that if it were not for you I should not be here. And I want to tell you how much I love you." (Mr. Lucey had been one of Calvin Coolidge's earliest supporters in his first try at political office.)

Children brought up in a farming community absorb without thinking the great facts of life and death. Babies were born at home, the family cow was led down the lane to Farmer Jones' bull and in due time there would be a soft-eyed calf and plenty of milk to drink. The sow under the barn in her pen was there to see, lying on her side with numberless piglets attached to rows of teats. There was a matter of fact air about reproduction and birth, it was a part of life. Old age too, was a part of life in the village. Grandparents too feeble to carry on at the old place came to live with married children and the boys and girls would have some responsibility to see that they were amused and cared for. In return the children would hear of life in the old days, of Indian raids and long ago battles and on stormy days learn how to crochet and knit and to piece a quilt. (Both boys and girls learned these skills; young Calvin's quilt still covers the spoolbed in the shed bedroom.) The sick were nursed at home and died in a warm downstairs room next to the kitchen. Neighbor women laid out the body, the village carpenter fashioned the plain coffin. Death was a familiar companion. "He made the pleasantest looking corpse I ever did see," was a cheerful remark in a Plymouth Notch diary.

Calvin Coolidge experienced all this in his boyhood. He learned to respect those older than himself for their insight and wisdom, to admire them for the way in which they'd lived their lives in an upright and honorable manner, owing nothing to any man. There was no separation of

The old were cared for at home. Aunt Mede in old age had a companion to live with in the large Coolidge farm house. CCMF

the teenagers from the rest of the community; the young were expected to learn from the elders living with them, then to take their place in turn. All ages felt a close association with each other. It was Calvin's duty as a grandson to ease the long dying of his grandfather. Calvin Galusha had lived a long and fruitful life; one could not be overwhelmed that the old man had gone to his just rewards.

But to have his beautiful young mother die! It was too frightful to be borne. But it had to be borne and the terrible ache buried deep inside him. Five years later almost to the day, Abbie, his closest companion, fell ill and died. He treated her death in the same stoic manner; that is how death must be handled, how any overwhelming emotion must be treated, bury it deep inside. Calvin never forgot those harshest of lessons.

Calvin started school in 1877 when he was only five years old, the youngest child in the Notch schoolhouse. His mother had already taught him to read. In the days before regional schools and fleets of busses, one room schools were dotted about a township. Plymouth at one time had as many as seventeen school districts, each district being an autonomous unit, raising money to maintain its own school and making arrangements to hire and board a teacher. It was felt necessary to have a school within walking distance for each child even if it was a long walk. Calvin was fortunate, for the Notch school, the 9th district, was just up the road beyond his house. It was built of rough-cut granite, the classic one-room school beloved of poets, a bare room fitted with crude wooden benches nailed to the floor. The amenities were sparse, a box stove in the middle around which the children were allowed to stand when the temperature outside dropped below zero. One year when the thermometer registered -20 degrees, young Calvin wrote in his diary, "Went to school as usual. It is a cold place I tell you." No running water of course, the back house was in the ell where the wood was stored, drinking water supplied in a pail filled each morning from a nearby house and drunk with a tin dipper. No-one felt deprived, this was what the children were used to in their own homes.

Although hill country folk knew the value of education, the work of the farm had to come first. Older children were needed at home and the school terms must be shaped to fit the farm year. The year Calvin began, school didn't start until December 17th. Often the winter term would end in late February so that the farmers could have plenty of hands for the sugar season. Sometimes there would be a summer and fall term but the number of terms and their dates was up to the wishes of each district.

Teachers were young men and women usually just out of school themselves and seldom taught more than two terms in succession. The requirements for becoming a teacher were minimal, merely an examination before the school superintendent. Calvin himself took the test at the age of thirteen and bright sister Abbie when she was only twelve actually taught a term in a nearby school! The main qualification for a teacher was to keep order, a male teacher having to be prepared to thrash any boy in the school, according to a school mate of Calvin's.

Schoolmastering was a hard task, the pay pitiful, living conditions often humiliating. Ernest Carpenter who was the Notch school teacher for the winter term of '84-'85 recorded that the pay for two terms was $159.70 including board at $37.70. Often a teacher was asked to "board around," staying a short time with the family of each pupil according to the number of children in each family. Schoolmaster Carpenter said that sometimes the family with the greatest number of children was not the most agreeable place to stay! Another means of providing board was to bid for the privilege, the teacher going to the lowest bidder. John Coolidge, in the days when he tried schoolmastering, told Ernest Carpenter that when he was teaching at Pinney Hollow school they bid him down to a farmer at twenty-five cents a week. No wonder the young teachers didn't stay long.

That first winter Calvin found himself in a room with twenty-three others ranging from his five years to adolescents of eighteen for country schools in those days were ungraded. It must have taken an extremely able person not only to be able to keep order but to be able to teach at all. Carpenter said no-one knew of the difficulties of teaching in an ungraded school; on the other hand Miss Ruth Aldrich of Plymouth Notch, teacher for many years, said she enjoyed every moment of her long and productive time in country schools. Calvin Coolidge said, "My teachers were young women from neighboring communities…They were all intelligent, of good character, and interested in their work. I do not feel that the quality of their instruction was in anyway inferior."

With the older students helping the little ones, who in turn listened to their elders, the teacher managed to work the eight grades through reading and spelling, arithmetic and algebra, United States history and civil government, geography and history of Vermont not to speak of Spencerian writing and Conant's parsing. At the end of eight years at the Notch school, Calvin Coolidge said later that he'd mastered the basics and was prepared to enter the larger world of Black River Academy in nearby Ludlow.

How did the schoolmates of the future President remember him, those Kavanaughs and Browns? Albert Sargent, an early schoolmate, interviewed when his old friend was in the White House said, "He wasn't particularly brilliant or otherwise at school. He was neither popular nor unpopular…He wasn't a leader in anything." A steady, methodical student, he ranked in the first half dozen in a school of thirty pupils. Ernest Carpenter remembered a red-headed, blue-eyed boy, slight of build and with a nasal twang that even then caused hilarity when his schoolmates tried to imitate him. He might have responded with a faint smile and a droll quip, the sort that became his trademark in later years. Jennie Chamberlain who helped out in the Coolidge household remembered Calvin's drawled response to a request to please wash his particularly dirty hands and a smudged face, "I don't know about that. I've known people to get drowned in water."

He was not a boisterous youth engaging in puppy-like scrambles with others but he was a tease, a trait that remained with him all his life. Once

Calvin Coolidge attended this school, one of seventeen in the town. CCMF

he persisted too long with a Kavanaugh girl, throwing water down her neck until she tackled Calvin and thoroughly thrashed him.

In the winter, to broaden the curriculum of the students and to entertain the community, a Lyceum would often be held, an institution to foster debates, put on plays or recitals. Favorite plays were well-worn shows such as *Under the Laurels* or *Among the Breakers*, guaranteed not to leave a dry eye in the house. Or a stage-struck adolescent might declaim *The Wreck of the Hesperus* with carefully chosen gestures. When a minstrel show was on the bill, Calvin was always given the position of end man for his ability to come up with a quick remark at the appropriate time.

Typical one-room school interior. Five year olds in front, teenagers in back.

All ages helped but it was a hard job for the teacher to keep order at times. VHS

The overwhelming favorite at a Lyceum was a debate, enticing hard-working farmers to drive long miles to attend or participate. Weighty subjects such as female suffrage and capital punishment were discussed with vigor until the most minute bones of the statement had been laid bare. This was a pastime that Calvin enjoyed and it is said that his later proficiency in speaking in a clear, understandable manner was gained in these village debates.

Though the usual boy's rough housing did not suit him, he was a typical child of the countryside in his rambles into the hills with friends, skating on the little ponds and trying to entice a brookie from the clear mountain streams.

It was always understood that fishing and rambling came only after farm chores were done. And in summer that meant the arduous and seemingly never ending task of haying.

Mowing machines began to be seen in the 1850s and by the time Calvin Coolidge was able to do a real day's work they were in common use in the hills of Vermont. Relieved of one of the most demanding of jobs, cutting the grass with a scythe, the farmer could get his hay in much quicker and in better condition. The advent of the hay rake and the tedder which kicked the hay out to dry faster, made the work easier but hay making in Vermont was always a time-consuming, worrisome season. It went on all summer until

The Vice-President comes back to mow his father's fields. FL

46

the hay mows were crammed full. But there was fine satisfaction in doing a neat job of mowing, watching the grass fall clearly under the blade in shining swaths, the sweet smell of the curing hay. Calvin on top of the hay wagon took pride in building the load just so, placing each forkful as it was pitched up to him so that when the wagon rolled into the barn, the hay could be pitched off in the same pattern. Pitching off up to the hay-mows was just about the hottest work this side of Tophet. High under the eaves there was no breeze, the hayseeds clung to the sweaty bodies but what immense satisfaction there was in getting the last load in just before the threatening thunderstorm broke! There was pleasure just in standing in the doorway, watching the rain slashing down, knowing that the precious wagonload was safe, and that, once more, the cattle would be well-fed in the coming winter. And if the cattle were well-fed it followed that the farm folk would be, too.

Next, corn had to be cut and husked. But that was a chore that could be turned into a party, a corn husking bee, where the lucky husker who got a red ear could kiss a girl. Apples must be picked and potatoes dug for storage. The able farmer had all this in hand by October. Then everyone took time to draw a deep breath and think of getting the house battened down for winter. Just before Thanksgiving the chickens and turkeys had to be killed and gotten ready for market and then it was the pig's time to

The neighborhood reaper-binder made its rounds in the fall. VHS

In the summer cows were often milked outside.
Below; Hill-country women in the 80's were still spinning wool for clothing. VHS

A long sweep made drawing water from the well easier.
At the blacksmith's, below, a boy could watch the smith
work wonders at his forge. VHS

be butchered. They had been fattening all summer on slops and skim milk left over from the butter making. The smoker was fired and the brine tubs readied. If it was cold enough the meat might be wrapped in cloths, put up somewhere like the edge of a roof where the animals couldn't get at it and frozen. When the frozen meat was packed in hay it would keep all winter. The housewife got out the family recipe for sausage and attended to the messy chore of rendering the fat which would be used to make soft soap, guaranteed to take the skin off your hands.

Thanksgiving was a regular old fashioned feast, the most New England of holidays. It was a time of family reunions, of cousins playing outdoors out of the way of the elders. The men gathered in the barnyard to examine the corn, discuss the action of a likely colt or perhaps, surreptitiously sample a bit of hard cider. The women, of course, were hard at work in the kitchen, basting fowl, peeling squash, setting the table and hoping that this year's pickles were as good as last's.

When it got really cold and promised to stay that way, it was "killing time" and the steer was slaughtered, his stark carcass hanging from a rafter until he could be turned into chunks in the salting tubs.

Christmas in New England for many years was regarded by the Puritan settlers as "too Popish" and was treated as just another working day. As late as 1835 young Pamela Brown of Plymouth Notch records in her diary for December twenty-fifth that she "…staid at Marcia's all day and finished the spencer." Perhaps it was the influence of Queen Victoria's German husband with his love of decorated trees, but by the time Calvin was old enough to enjoy Christmas it had become respectable even in New England. There was a village celebration for the school children at the church with a tree from the woods and gifts and cookies, and in the houses, Calvin Coolidge says in his autobiography, "…stockings were hung and the spruce tree lighted in the symbol of Christian faith and love."

During the winter the task of cutting the next year's supply of wood took over, for all the heating and cooking was done with firewood. Hyde Leslie worked for the James S. Brown family of the Notch for almost seven months in 1887 and kept a journal during that time. A typical winter entry goes thus: "I split what wood I sawed yesterday on the Hensey Lot also cut a little more beside helping C. W. Blanchard to make a road in the Deep Hard Snow so he could get the steers to the wood pile…Chas and Henry drew 4 foot wood with the Steers today, 3 small loads, one cord."

Like the ordeal of haying there was a good deal of satisfaction in the wood operation. It was the only work that could be done outside in the short winter days. It was a chance to get away from the confines of the house and barn and out into the clean black and white of the wood lot. The

Winter roads were not plowed but rolled smooth for horse-drawn sleighs. VHS

Below; John Coolidge tries out the new-fangled Ludlow motor stage. Alas, it kept sliding into ditches and was soon abandoned. VDHP

chopper would have felled the trees selected for next year's fuel supply and trimmed off the branches. Then the team of oxen standing patiently waiting would be led to the thick butt end where a chain from their yoke would be hitched around the log and with a commanding "Wa hush!" the log would be drawn into a convenient spot. When enough had been collected, someone with a few hours time, armed with a buck saw, would saw the logs into four foot lengths which could then be carried by sled to the house, cut and split again, then piled neatly to spend the summer drying. Then of course the wood had to be shifted once more into the woodshed where a youngster like Calvin would come to replenish the woodbox everyday. Farmers were judged by the manner in which they stacked their wood. A careful, capable man would insist that his pile be stacked just so with all the sawn edges absolutely straight as a well made wall. One farmer in Hartland Four Corners, a town east of Plymouth, amused himself and his neighbors every year by building his wood pile in the shape of a fort complete even to gun ports with wooden cannons carefully aimed.

Of all the seasons that ruled the life of the hill farmer, sugar time was the one that every one looked forward to. Eagerly the first signs of the season were looked for, the lengthening days, warms days, cold nights and the first faint reddening of the tips of the maple branches. When the farmer had decided the time had come, a road would be broken out to the sugar-bush. There, snowshoes would be donned, and armed with augers and spiles, with a sled following piled high with buckets, the men would wade to each tree. Boring a hole with the auger, a spile would be hammered into the tree, a bucket fetched from the sled and hung on the spile. It was hard work, but the crew would be imbued with a sense of happiness knowing that the long hard days of winter were past…Vermont's lovely spring couldn't be far away.

In the meantime the sugar-house had been readied; last fall an enormous amount of wood had been piled nearby. The smokestack had been fitted together, the roof ventilators opened and the pans cleaned of any nests that a woodmouse may have made. The trees responding to the warming season, commenced to push the sap upwards, some of it trickling down into the buckets. In a day or so they would be nearly filled, then the gathering began. Plodding on snow shoes through the snow, wooden yoke across shoulders, the gatherers went from tree to tree emptying the buckets into the two dangling at the ends of the yoke and then to the gathering tank drawn on a sled. It was almost a game to see who could collect the most sap without spilling while climbing up and down the steep slopes of the sugarbush. Calvin took pride in his dexterity and in the carefully fashioned yoke he had made, still hanging in his father's workshed. He took pride too in the amount of clear amber syrup he boiled down from the sap for only the most careful person was allowed to boil; an instant's carelessness could ruin not only the laboriously gathered sap but burn up an expensive pan as well. His father said Calvin could get more syrup than anyone, high praise indeed for a master sugar-maker himself. The syrup was taken to the house and boiled down again into maple sugar, two thousand pounds in good years! Most of the sugar was stored in tin pails but many housewives poured some into little molds of fancy shapes to be given at Christmas or sent to far away relatives in the Middle West.

At the end of the season, sugaring-off in Vermont was almost as festive as Thanksgiving or Christmas. Anything that was an excuse for a party was welcome in a snowbound village. All that was necessary for a sugar-on-snow party was plenty of syrup at the boil, lots of fresh clean snow, a good supply of raised doughnuts and pickles and enough people in a mood to celebrate the end of the sugar season and the beginning of spring.

When the spiles and buckets had been collected from the bush and washed, the sugarhouse was closed for the summer, and it was time to "fix fence." Neighbors whose boundaries ran together would set a time to meet to repair their common fence with each other's help. It was an opportunity to "visit," to see how the back pastures were faring and to discuss the doings at the recent town meeting. They would find gaps where the snow or last summer's heifers had made an opening which could be repaired on the spot by heaving back into place a few stones. Barbed wire was just coming into use then but was used mostly on the treeless and

Sugaring was a time of delight; it meant the long winter was over, Vermont's beautiful spring was on its way. Everyone lent a hand. VHS

stoneless plains. The frugal New Englander would consider it almost a crime to spend good money on barbed wire when he already had more fence material than he knew what to do with, stones.

When the first green crept over the hill and the fences were all fixed, it was "turn out time." It was a time when all halted their tasks for awhile; farm wives left the clothesline, children too small to be in school watched when the calves and cows, sheep and lambs were let out in the pasture for the first time that year. Since fall they had been penned or tied in dark barns and sheds or confined to small, muddy enclosures. They would stand for a moment, savoring the spring air as if surprised to find themselves outdoors, then perhaps an old dry leaf skittered across the grass. In an instant they were off, bucking, galloping, their tails lifted high over their backs, sedate cow mothers acting like heifers, nearly twisting themselves in two with spring joy. Soon they would fall to eating the new grass and everyone went back to work, but smiling a little inside.

Then everything had to be done at once; the smelly job of getting dung out of the pigpen, the manure from under the cow tie-ups where it had been accumulating all winter, not to mention that in the hen house. Sheep had to be sheared, fields plowed and harrowed and planted at just the right time. How proud Calvin was when he was allowed to plow by himself! It was a heavy task but the slender boy found he had the ability

In spring everything had to be done at once, fences fixed, animals turned out to pasture. VHS   *Right; Calvin Coolidge helps with plowing.* CCMF

to keep the cumbersome plow in the earth and to guide the oxen at the same time. At the end of the day he looked back and saw with pride his furrows lying straight and true. He had done a man's job.

Then there was the kitchen garden and the flower garden, for almost every house had a flower garden and before anyone could catch a breath it was time to begin haying!

So did the farm year turn on the slow wheel of the seasons. For those who were strong, for those who loved the quiet rhythm of the year it was a most satisfactory way to spend a life. For others it was a confining prison. A young Plymouth man threw down his milking stool one evening; "That's the last cow I'll ever milk," and off he went to Massachusetts. But it was a fine way to grow up. "It would be hard to imagine better surroundings for the development of a boy than those I had," said President Coolidge. For one thing it gave a girl or a boy a sense of responsibility. Unless the woodbox was filled the kitchen would be cold and breakfast late. If hens or calves were forgotten they might take sick. A farm child grew up knowing that he or she had an important part in maintaining the life of the family and without their help the family would suffer.

But there were lots of good times for these hill country children, amusements that the hills and ponds afforded, homemade good times. When the little brooks swelled with fall rains so they overflowed their banks, country children prayed for a cold spell to freeze the surface. After school they'd put a tentative testing toe on the edge to see if the ice held but knowing that if anyone did go through, the water would be only a foot or so deep. What a cold business it was getting those skates on, sitting on the damp ground struggling with blue fingers to fasten the stiff leather straps. But how effortless their motion once they got over feeling wobbly, and what exciting games of snap the whip were played on the meadow ponds. "Skated with Thomas," wrote Calvin in his schoolboy diary, day after day. His skates still await their young owner, unused now for nearly a hundred years. Thomas Moore, one of those who spelled their name with an 'e', who lived just down the lane toward Grandfather Coolidge, was near Calvin's age and a boon companion. "Went hunting with Thomas." Like all country boys, Calvin had a rifle and felt impelled to shoot at birds and woodchucks and other small mammals but with some sense of compassion. Perhaps it was Galusha's love of animals inherited by his grandson. "Shot at the bluejays who were eating the corn. It seemed a pity to aim at the pretty things." Indeed, all his life he liked having animals about him. He speaks fondly of a "pretty little heifer" and on stormy days as a small boy used to dress-up his patient cat in baby clothes. Stepmother Carrie shared his love of felines, her beautiful orange cat and a handsome tiger are still remembered by neighbors. Later, the President's "Tige" was a well known inhabitant of the White House, her master carrying her about draped like a fur piece across his shoulders. The Coolidge dogs were always noteworthy news items, not to speak of Rebecca, the raccoon, who dined at the White House on Mrs. Coolidge's bathroom floor on shrimp and chicken.

As the Vermont winter deepened, the snows came, covering the hills with a white blanket. "Feb. 2. We had a good time to school as usual and had a good time sleding." The road that ran down past the school and homestead made a satisfactorily perilous ride on the bobsled, which managed to turn over near Grandfather Moor's house, spilling children in a glorious tangle at least once every afternoon.

*The family gathered around the kitchen table,
a warm symbol of comfort and well-being.* VDHP

Then, all too soon, the cold sun would sink behind the mountains and it would be time to go home to devour some cookies and milk and to be sure the woodbox was filled.

Calvin Coolidge must have, in later days, remembered with nostalgia the quiet evenings after supper. The dishes would have been washed and put back on the table upside down, ready for morning. It would be pleasant in the warm sitting room lit by a kerosene lamp. The children studied or listened to someone reading aloud while mother attended to her endless task of darning socks.

After sugaring, in April, when the leaves on the maple trees were still as small as a field mouse's ear, was the best time for exploring. A boy shinnying up a tree on top of a hill could see into the distance forever. Plymouth brooks held their own excitement; Money Brook for instance, where once a band of counterfeiters had a camp. One of the favorite spots was where a large rock split a small brook so that one stream flowed south toward the Black River and one flowed north in the opposite direction. Why, if someone moved the boulder just a fraction you could send more water south and the Ottauquechee would have less. Like the boulder, it wouldn't take much to change the whole direction of a person's life.

The Calvin Coolidge myth has it that he was particularly abrupt in his speech, almost rudely so. Claude Fuess in his book relates that Coolidge confessed in later years to his friend Frank Stearns, "When I was a little fellow, as long ago as I can remember, I would go into a panic if I heard strange voices in the kitchen. I felt I just couldn't meet the people and shake hands with them. Most of the visitors would sit with Father and Mother in the kitchen, and the hardest thing in the world was to have to go through the kitchen door and give them a greeting." Now, he said, he was all right with old friends, "but everytime I meet a stranger, I've got to go through the old kitchen door, back home, and it's not easy." Timid as he was with unknown faces, as a boy he was as gregarious as any self-assured village youth. "Went up to Alfred's tonight and had a good time." (Alfred Moore's stone dwelling housed three daughters and a parlor organ). "Last day of school. We had a party at home tonight and had a very good time." Undoubtedly, Abbie, with her lively outgoing nature, helped her shy brother unbend and reveal his essentially warm affectionate nature. Certainly his boyhood diaries reveal that he liked to be included in every event taking place in the Notch and later on, in Ludlow.

There was plenty going on in the Vermont hill-towns in the late 19th century, especially in the winter when people had more leisure. Victoria Josphine's diary, just before she married John Coolidge, lists an astonishing number of affairs she attended in January; from parties to Lyceums, one almost every night, a record to daunt the most restless teenager of today.

Stella McWain, lively fifteen year old sister of housekeeper Martha, was asked by John Coolidge to live in the Coolidge house and be a companion for ten year old Abbie the winter Calvin went off to Black River Academy. "It was the best winter of my life," she said years later remembering the dances and sociables held that year. She particularly relished the "kitchen junkets" when the boys would clear a kitchen of tables, chairs and dressers and when "Uncle John" Wilder would come over with his fiddle. The houses usually chosen for the dance would have an organ which Stella would play along with Uncle John's fiddle. "Money Musk," the "Soldier's Joy" and the "Devil's Dream" were favorite dance tunes then and again when the Plymouth Hometown Dance Band went on its campaign tour in 1924.

Abbie didn't dance said Stella, but there was usually a card game going, "Double King Pede" being very popular at the time.

Oyster suppers at the church were favorite entertainments of the time too, and for the younger folk nothing was more fun than a candy pull at a friend's house, especially when some sticky strands were sure to be caught in a girl's hair!

The icy stillness of a full moon in January was the best time to have a hay ride. Everyone crowded together under buffalo robes, and if a boy was lucky and smart he made sure to sit next to a particularly pretty girl and hold her hand. No-one ever forgot how sweet the strains of "Aunt Dinah's Quilting Party" sounded as the sled glided over the snow, casting a long moving shadow in the moonlight.

Albert Moore lived nearby in this house. He owned an organ and had three daughters; the best house for a party! CCMF

In May, Memorial Day was observed with a parade by the school children, the girls all dressed in white, carrying flowers to the cemetery to decorate the soldier's graves. When Calvin was growing up in the '80s, Civil War veterans were middle-aged men, living reminders of one of the momentous episodes in American history. Veteran Levi Lynds lived near the Coolidge house and after chores Calvin used to walk across the meadow to listen to Levi's stories of the war. Blanche Brown said that this companionship probably sparked his first interest in history.

The Plymouth Notch Sunday School picnic was another festivity centered around children. The year Calvin's mother died, his father organized the event. He had an organ moved on a wagon to a nearby grove

Sunday School Picnic: Calvin, encircled, father John stands hat in

hand, sixth from left in the back row. Abbie is behind the post. CCMF

where the boys and girls and a goodly number of grownups picnicked and sang and wandered about to pick anemones and violets. As was customary, a group picture was taken and shows chubby Abbie in an elaborate hat and Calvin looking small and rather forlorn.

When Old Home Day rolled around sometime in the summer, the much travelled organ was boosted onto a wagon again and set up on a platform decorated in red, white and blue bunting. Usually the event was held down at the Plymouth Union in a maple grove (still standing today), and was attended by local inhabitants and by town folks who had moved away. Nostalgic for their childhood homes, they had made an effort to come back and visit with friends and to eat vast amounts of baked beans and potato salad and home-made ice cream. The Coolidges could always be counted on to bring lots of ice cream; they owned a two quart machine which took a deal of cranking. The folks listened to talented Plymouthites sing or play the violin and there'd be speeches and sometimes the Ludlow band would give a concert and usually, after a spell of quiet digestion, the men would play baseball.

Sometimes in the summer, a circus came to Rutland and that meant getting up at three in the morning in order to be over the mountains in time to see the circus parade.

At the Windsor County Fair in September one could see the fastest horses, the biggest pumpkins and the fattest pigs. VHS

At summer's end it was fair time. Town fairs were local events like the one held in the meadow back of Grandfather Moor's barn. But the dearest wish of every Plymouth child was to be able to go to the biggest and best of all the county fairs, their own county, Windsor County Fair held in Woodstock. That meant awakening early too, to be able to get a good place to leave the horse and buggy not too far from the ring. Children too excited to fall asleep on the long morning ride, would clamber down from the back seat, given a judiciously doled out number of coins and told to be back in time for the basket lunch mother had put up the night before. Father, after attending to the comfort of the horse, went straight off to see the latest in farm equipment and mother went right to Floral Hall where she planned to meet friends not seen since last year's fair and to look at afghans and antimacassars. No-one wanted to miss Vegetable Hall where the biggest orange pumpkins and the clearest ruby-colored jellies imaginable were on show. And there was time to see J.J. Nutting's exhibit of the latest in caskets; you never knew when one might be needed. Afternoon was the time when the horse races were held and everyone remembered the year when L.C. Udall got so excited that he dropped dead right in the stands. And to top it all off aerialist Madame Leone was on hand with her hot air balloon to make a perilous ascent! After that there was nothing to do but climb into the buggy and head for home, tired children asleep, mother and father in front, their heads filled with plans for a new horse-drawn rake and a pattern for a lovely shawl.

But best of all days, the one that caused the most excitement, was the Glorious Fourth. For months boys had been hoarding money, getting enough pennies, nickels and dimes together to send out an order to Ohio to the Brazil Fireworks Co. $1.67 would buy enough four-inch salutes and Chinese firecrackers to last all day if a fellow was careful and didn't fire off everything at once. Small rockets and bombs (tissue-wrapped balls with caps mixed with pebbles) made a most satisfactory noise. For a few days afterwards small boys claimed they couldn't hear their mothers calling, their ears rang so. But this was small beer compared to the annual Plymouth cannon contest. The cannon was the result of a surge of patriotic fervor in the late 1830's, paid for by public subscription of Plymouth folk and cast at Isaac Tyson's foundry. It had been first fired to announce the result of President William Henry Harrison's election, "Tippecanoe and Tyler Too" in 1840. But which village should have possession? Over the years the boys of the Union and the Notch had vied for the honor of firing on the Fourth, until the issue was settled once and for all in 1892. No-one is exactly sure after all these years who was in the little raiding party from the Notch that crept down in the very early hours of the morning before the Fourth, but it is thought that Calvin Coolidge, along with Dell Ward and John Wilder, was on hand. Quietly they drew the 500 pound cannon from its place at the Union and

John Wilder and the famous Plymouth cannon. VHS

dragged it up the steep slope to the Notch, no small job. Some master mind decided to hide it behind the pile of manure in the basement of the Wilder barn. Early on the morning of the Fourth, it was dragged up behind the big doors. When the doors were opened, floor planks were lifted up, rolling out the cannon without any of the crew being seen. A long lanyard was pulled, the cannon announced the dawn of the glorious day with a full throated roar that rattled every window in the village. Before the bewildered sleepers could gather their wits, the cannon was quickly drawn inside with a long rope and the barn doors closed. Swiftly it was swabbed out, reloaded and rolled out again to proclaim that the Republic still stood.

A lookout cannily placed at the top of the Notch announced the charge of the angry Union boys. They had heard the distant thunder, discovered their prize missing and came running up the road to be met by John Wilder. "I'll fight the first of you and then everyone in turn!" Faced with such fierceness, the Union forces prudently retreated, and the cannon has remained at the Notch ever since. That afternoon Calvin Coolidge, by now a young Amherst student, gave a stirring speech on the glories of independence with every appearance of solemn good behavior.

In the 1880's if you wanted to go somewhere, to the store or school or to the post office, you walked. If the trip was longer, it meant harnessing the horse. It might be that the horse was needed for raking hay that day or he might be lame. In that case you walked or stayed home. Trips beyond the confines of Plymouth were not undertaken lightly and were rare in young Calvin's life. One he barely remembered was when he was three and Grand-father Galusha took him and his mother to Montpelier to see his father who was a member of the Vermont General Assembly. They told Calvin afterward that Galusha sat him in the big, black, leather Speaker's chair; but he remembered only the snarl of Vermont's last catamount, safely stuffed and in a glass case, still to be seen at the Vermont Historical Society in Montpelier.

There was every good reason to go down to Bennington to see President Benjamin Harrison dedicate the new Battle of Bennington monument in the summer of 1891. How many times does a Vermonter get to see the President of the United States? Calvin went down with his father for the ceremony and truly Vermont has not seen its like since. There were hours and hours of full-blown oratory, and miles of bands and a sixty-foot arch of canvas, painted to look like stone, from which little girls dropped roses on the President's head as he rode in a carriage pulled by four white horses. Of the President, Calvin said, "As I looked on him and realized that he personally represented the glory and dignity of the United States I wondered how it felt to bear so much responsibility and little thought I should ever known."

Battle of Bennington Day, when Calvin saw the President. BM

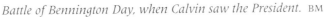

III

SCHOOL DAYS

THE winter Calvin was thirteen years old, he had finished his studies at the stone school house. For many children that was all the education they would ever have. Most hill country families needed their labor and any wages they could earn. Calvin's father wanted his children to have at least some terms at his old school, Black River Academy. Of course it meant a long trip of twelve miles down to Ludlow and then there was the tuition as well as the board to consider. It would be about $7 a term for the school, and board and room would probably be another $3 a week, around $150

Left; Ludlow, Vermont, in the 80's. VHS
*Above; Black River Academy, where the
future President struggled with algebra.* FL

for a year. But John Coolidge considered Calvin's education a good invest-
ment, so on a bitterly cold morning in February in 1886 the little household
arose at 5 a.m. to see Calvin off on his first great adventure. He was dressed
in his "good" clothes, his two small handbags in the back of the sleigh along
with a calf bound for the Boston market. John Coolidge's words of advice to
his son as he left home on his own for the first time were, "Calvin, if you
study hard and are a good boy, maybe sometime you'll go to Boston too, but
the calf will get there first." Calvin never forgot how he felt that first morning. The memories of it flooded over him whenever he started out on a new
enterprise, particularly the morning when he left Plymouth for the White
House. "Going to the Academy meant a complete break with the past and
entering a new and untried field, larger and more alluring than the past,
among unknown scenes and unknown people."

  The three story building from which he graduated still stands in its
Victorian monumentality in the middle of Ludlow, a small manufacturing
town. Although he spoke afterward about the excitement of the new

scenes, to be lifted so abruptly from his small familiar life in the Notch, must have been a shock. He never once thought of complaining; his father had decided he would go and that was that. The most he would do was to write in his diary such sentences as, "Have a good time down here but not as good as I expected." And, again, "I shall not be glad when I go back to school (he was at home for vacation) but should be more sorry if I could not go back."

He stoutly declared, "I have to study hard, am not homesick one bit." But the mysteries of algebra were hard going for the youngster from Plymouth School District Number Nine. "O, I shall be glad when algebra is done!" One of his classmates told of Calvin's coming to his room at night for help in the subject and saying solemnly to the boarding house proprietress, "Well, I've come down to help Henry do his algebra again." He so convinced the woman she asked Henry if he was failing in the subject.

Black River Academy, or BRA as it was called, did not provide dormitories for its students, they had to find their own room and board. Calvin lived with a number of families who took in students, and he and his fellow pupils seem to have enjoyed being away from their father's supervisory eyes. These were children of hard working farmers and knew that their families were making sacrifices to send them to school. They didn't expect much excitement; after supper Calvin would take a walk with his roommates and then get back to the rooming house to study. But high spirits couldn't be repressed. "We had a time with Loren tonight. We got him to bed with George and when Fred came home, twitched him out and turned a pitcher of water on him." Evidently Calvin sometimes had to sleep with Loren, who, he complained, rolled up in all the bedclothes so that Calvin had to "sleep cold." He also complained that Loren hadn't washed once the whole term and Calvin couldn't get Loren near the wash basin.

After a winter of "sleeping cold" and pitcher pouring, Calvin was often bothered by colds, a foretaste of delicate health in later years. "I did not study much of any this afternoon. I do not feel like study. I got me a bottle of Woods Sarsaparilla today. I hope it will make me feel more lively. I am sick with a cold tonight. Am troubled to breathe."

And then when April came, there was spring fever to contend with. "Had pretty good lessons but I can not study much for I look outdoors so for if I tried to study I am thinking of something else. So I stared up street all afternoon."

Compared with Plymouth Notch, Ludlow was a beehive of activities and events. Calvin attended an opera and a lecture series with a magic lantern, and an ox roast that had the town talking for days. His mother's older sister Sarah Pollard lived in nearby Proctorsville, a warm hearted woman who enjoyed having her nephew come for weekends when his father could not make the long drive from the Notch. Proctorsville offered some lively entertainment too, for Calvin notes in his diary, "Went down to Proctorsville tonight to a dance. It was good too. Did not get to bed till 12 o'clock. Shall not tell the faculty I went down." When one is a teenager it's hard to remember a grandmother's injunction against dances.

A pleasant day in Proctorsville, a few miles from Ludlow. VHS

Organized sports did not exist then, only a sort of primitive baseball called "one o' cat" or "tossball." Blanche Brown Bryant says in her *Calvin Coolidge As I Knew Him*, that he always played "fully and neatly dressed and wore his derby hat.

Calvin was often too busy to play one o' cat in his derby hat; his father had urged him to get a job. On Saturdays Calvin worked in a carriage shop, making wooden toys earning a little money which his father immediately put in a savings account, so that Calvin might understand how money earned more money. It was a lesson his son never forgot.

For all his enjoyment of new companionship, Calvin missed the young person he felt closest to, sister Abbie. He kept urging the family to let her come to BRA. "What do you think about Abbie's coming to school here this spring? I think she had better, … It takes one term to get used to the ways and know what you are about, before you can do very good work."

The lively red-head came down to Ludlow the fall of 1888 and as Calvin knew she would, made not only a fine scholastic record but with her outgoing personality made many friends as well. In March of 1890 the bad luck of the Coolidges struck the little family again. Abbie was taken very ill and carried back to Plymouth. For a week she suffered what one of her doctors later told the President was appendicitis. In 1890 nothing was known of it except to call it "inflammation of the bowels." When her condition became critical, Calvin was called home to watch her die. She was only fourteen years old. "The memory of the charm of her presence...will always abide with me."

A month later in a letter from Ludlow to his father, he was worrying about his graduation clothes. "Would you be willing that I should get a suit of clothes this spring? These that I have I have worn every day for almost two terms...I know my expenses are very large this spring and will get along without a new suit if you think best." He had inquired about the cost and found one at the Ludlow Clothing House that suited and cost $17. He ended the letter saying, "It is lonely here without Abbie."

In spite of anxieties about his studies Calvin did well enough in his class, partly through his disciplined study habits, and because he was inspired by two of his teachers, Principal George Sherman and Miss M. Belle Chellis. "It was under their teaching that I first learned of the grandeur of the ancient civilizations that grew up around the Mediterranean...They gave me a vision of the world when it was young..." Under their tutelage he had been well schooled in Greek and Latin, languages whose influence can be detected in his later speeches.

Calvin carefully poses in his graduation suit. VDHP

Left; Black River Academy Class of 1890. JC

Without Abbie to see him, Calvin graduated from Black River Academy on May 23, 1890. The class of five boys and four girls marched down an aisle decorated with potted plants and flowers and listened while the Rev. J.B. Reardon of the Universalist Church offered prayer and classmate Asa Albert Sargent delivered the Salutatory. It was a long program but the audience had patience and persistence to wait until J. Calvin Coolidge, secretary of the class, gave a historical resumé of the influence of oratory in the great moments of history. "This oration was masterly in its conception and arrangement", declared the *Vermont Tribune*. In the evening everyone attended a commencement concert given by the Temple Quartette of Boston assisted by the Whistling Soloist, Miss Ella Chamberlain.

After such an outstanding day there was nothing left but to say goodbye and return to the Notch and the summer's farm work. He must have returned home pondering in his mind what would now be the course of his life, like the little brook that flowed in two directions. There was no doubt that he didn't intend to become a farmer as his Grandfather Galusha had wished. He had discovered the joys of the world that books had opened to him and hoped that perhaps he could go on to college after a post-graduate course at Exeter or Andover. It would be striking out on an entirely different path, for no Coolidge had ever gone to college. Except for John Garibaldi (Garry) Sargent, who graduated from Tufts in 1887, no-one from Plymouth had ever gone to college. If his father wished him to remain at the Notch as a storekeeper he would do it. But it was Principal George Sherman, the only well educated person Calvin had ever met, who suggested that Calvin should go to Amherst after taking a qualifying exam. Since BRA did not possess a college certificate, Calvin would have to go to Amherst for an exam in the classics, English and math. John Coolidge agreed to let his son try and drove him to Ludlow to catch the train. On his first trip by himself he caught a severe cold which grew so bad that half way through the exam period he had to give up and return home ignominiously. No doubt after such high hopes, he must have wondered if it might not be easier to just stay home and tend store. On the other hand he had liked what he had seen of the larger world beyond the Notch. He decided to keep sharp his literary teeth by reading the poems of Sir Walter Scott and to take another term at the Academy. In the meantime he worked at painting the inside of the store. It was his old Principal Sherman who again urged him to try for Amherst, this time by way of St. Johnsbury Academy which did grant a college certificate.

This time the plan worked and after the spring term, St. Johnsbury Academy awarded Calvin the right to enter Amherst as a freshman in the fall of 1891. That was also the year his father married Carrie Brown, a long-time neighbor in the Notch. "After being without a mother nearly seven years I was greatly pleased to find in her all the motherly devotion that she could have given me if I had been her own son."

So nineteen year old Calvin Coolidge went off to college. It was not an easy transition for the quiet shy youth. In a college dominated by fraternity life he was completely overlooked by the socially conscious young bloods. "I am in a pleasant place and like very much but suppose I shall like better as (I) become more acquainted, I don't seem to get acquainted

very fast however." He wasn't at Amherst to roister at fraternities, but it was certainly lonely. It was not until his junior year that he gained some recognition. Carrying a cane and wearing a silk hat bought especially for the occasion, he and his classmates had to race the length of the football field. The last seven men in had to buy a supper for the rest and give a speech. Calvin, one of the seven, had to speak on "Why I got stuck." In pantomime he pulled his pockets inside out to show how broke he was and said that plow horses weren't racers and that pitching hay was a poor

Young Coolidge at Amherst, neatly attired and suitably hatted. FL

way to train for foot races but reminded them, "Boys, remember the Good Book says that the first shall be last and the last, first." From then on he was regarded as a witty fellow and someone to befriend. In his last year he became a Phi Gamma Delta and for the rest of his life kept up his interest in the fraternity, one of the few organizations he ever joined.

In the summers he dutifully returned home to help on the farm. But youth, however hardworking, yearned for some contact with the opposite sex.

Most of Calvin Coolidge's biographers state that they could get no hint of any romantic attachments until the vivacious Grace Goodhue came on the scene. Certainly his autobiography reveals nothing of any boyish or adolescent loves. However, Blanche Brown Bryant says that he admired Plymouth's Lena Levey, but from afar, as she was "spoken for." Certainly Midge Gilson, living down by Black Pond, was an objective on his horse-back rides in his spare time. Midge, an accomplished violinist, was his choice as a companion on an adventurous trip to Ausable Chasm. Besides a Miss Clark of Keene whose sister lived in Ludlow, he courted a cousin of Blanche Brown's, a student at Smith College while he was in Amherst. He reportedly wooed her with bouquets but her heart was already pledged to another. Carrie Coolidge, devoted stepmother, worried about Calvin's lack of success in love affairs. "Calvin," she said, "would make a good husband if one could overlook his oddities."

Whatever his failures to secure one of these young ladies for a mate, in the end he won one of the most attractive and beguiling women ever to grace the White House. But that was in the future.

The promising young Northampton lawyer. VHS

IV

MARRIAGE AND
THE PRESIDENCY

More immediate was the question of what to do after graduation from college. He had it in mind to become a lawyer but hesitated to ask his father to finance three more years in law school. The tried and true method of "reading" under an established lawyer would do very well. He wrote former Governor William Dillingham asking for a place in his office in Montpelier, but the Governor was away and didn't answer Coolidge's letter at once. In the meantime Calvin heard of an opening in the law offices of Hammond and Field in Northampton, Massachusetts. Accordingly, he left Vermont. It is futile to speculate on what Calvin Coolidge's life would have been had he stayed in his native state but it is probable that the path to the White House would not have opened for him.

He duly became a lawyer but used the law as a stepping stone for politics, the career he really loved. Once, when asked, "What are your hobbies?," he shot back, "Holding office!"

The story of his progression from City Councilman to Governor of Massachusetts to the Presidency has been told many times, one of the great success stories of American history. He said this about his amazing career, "Some power that I little suspected in my student days took me in charge and carried me from the obscure neighborhood at Plymouth Notch to the occupancy of the White House."

Always smoothing his path was his wife, Grace Goodhue Coolidge, laughing at his quirks, charming those offended by Coolidge's seeming rudeness.

She was a Burlington, Vermont girl, high spirited, young and handsome. A story has it that a friend once dared her to swallow a whole peeled hard boiled egg. She got it down but almost choked in the process. A graduate of the University of Vermont she taught at the Clarke School for the Deaf in Northampton, Massachusetts. She first saw her future husband

Grace Goodhue in 1900. FL

when she looked up at the rooming house next door and saw a young man shaving in his union suit with his hat on. He was intrigued by her laughter and wangled an introduction to her. He explained that the hat was to keep an unruly lock of hair from getting in the way when he shaved.

Calvin fell in love immediately with Grace, while for her part she saw that the red-headed young lawyer concealed behind his impassive manner a sensitive, loving nature. They were married in 1905.

She could not have found her new life easy. He shared none of her love for music, theatre or baseball. She loved a good time; he went about in society with dogged glumness. He missed her when she was out, looking out of the window until she returned. Once when she stayed long at a tea party, he telephoned, "Grace, I've come home. You come home too."

He was extremely careful with his money, never owning a car, or his own house until he retired from the Presidency. Even in the White House he kept as careful an eye on expenditures as he did when they were first married and living on a young lawyer's income. He liked to prowl about the Presidential kitchens, opening refrigerator doors and checking the amount of food prepared. Six Virginia hams he thought too many for a party of sixty. The housekeeper did not relish his comments. Once when a large party was planned and the pantries were full of goodies, the President came down to see what was going on. "Looks like good cat and dog food to me." The staff was not pleased.

Governor and Mrs. Coolidge with sons John and Calvin, Jr.
Coolidge bought The Beeches, below, after retirement. Both VHS

The Coolidges at Plymouth. Grace Coolidge was one of the best dressed of First Ladies thanks, in large part, to her husband's surprisingly good eye for ladies clothes. CCMF

But in one respect he was a spendthrift; he loved to see his attractive wife well dressed. On his daily walks about Washington, he kept his eye on the shop windows. If a particularly fetching gown or hat (he loved bright colors and ribbons) caught his attention he would have them sent up to the White House for her approval. Certainly Grace Coolidge was one of the best dressed of First Ladies; Calvin Coolidge had excellent taste in clothes.

Whatever their differing temperaments they understood each other's sense of humor; she never failed to pick up his wry, straight-faced quips or put up with his practical jokes. He in turn knew he could get away with them with his understanding Grace. She was having a fitting one afternoon, a ball dress with a long white satin train. In walked the President straight over to where the dressmaker was on her knees. Without saying a word he solemnly walked right up the length of the train, ignoring the shrieks of the two women. Then he smiled and left the room. It was like the time when he first inherited the Presidential office and couldn't resist the impulse to push every bell on the desk at once to see what would happen. Grace always knew that he loved her with all his heart. "For almost a quarter of a century she has borne with my infirmities and I have rejoiced in her graces."

After he moved to Northampton and married, Calvin came back to Vermont only as a visitor; his concerns belonged to another state and finally to the country as a whole. But the ties to his childhood home were still strong and in particular those to his father. He came back whenever he could and saw to it that his sons, John and Calvin, spent their summers working on the farm as he had in his youth.

As he became known to the country, newspaper reporters began to recognize his uniqueness as a subject. They played upon his quaint background, his pithy remarks and strangely, for a private man, Coolidge did not mind being in the limelight. Only when he sensed a teasing note, such as the time he was photographed in his grandfather's smock and calfskin boots, did he become irritated. When the newspaper referred to his "fancy dress," he ruefully put aside the smock. "I have since been obliged to forego the comfort of wearing it." He complained that nobody called the King of England's kilt "fancy dress." The smock hangs still in the shed bedroom.

President Coolidge liked to wear his grandfather's hand-woven woolen smock at the farm. CCMF

*He relaxed in the summer doing farm chores, sharpening a
scythe,* VDHP *or gathering hay with father and the boys.* FL.

It was pleasant, too, to chat with his father, VHS, *or visit with Aunt Mary Wilder and talk about times gone by.* FL

Besmocked or not, the American people sensed in him something trustworthy, an honest quality, homespun and regular with which they could identify. But when that background was called "Lincolnesque" he objected. He wanted it known that his boyhood was a normal one, of a frugal, self-respecting industrious family, neither poverty stricken or affluent.

Always meticulously neat in his appearance he made no concession when indulging in his only outdoor sport, fishing. He kept on his suit coat, donned a pair of waders and kept his straw boater squarely on his head. It must be remembered that this was before the day when Americans felt they had to wear the correct "sport clothes" for each separate activity.

He had gotten a great deal of attention as governor of Massachusetts in his settling of the famous Boston Police Strike with the statement that "There is no right to strike against the public safety by anybody, anywhere, any time." His forthright action in this matter helped make him Vice-President in 1920.

Coolidge always enjoyed fishing, even when posing for the press. VHS

He didn't know that next day he'd be President. VHS

He was spending some weeks in the summer of 1923 with his father when President Harding, travelling on the West Coast, fell ill. But the reports on the sick man seemed encouraging so the Vice-President spent August 2nd digging out some rot from a maple in his father's front yard, ate supper and went to bed about nine o'clock.

In the middle of the night a message was received at the White River Junction, Vermont telegraph station that President Harding was dead. The news was telegraphed to Bridgewater where W.A. Perkins, in charge of the telephone office, got the message and raced up the winding road to the Notch, arriving around midnight. Banging on the door of the homestead Perkins woke the Colonel, a poor sleeper. He came to the screen door in bare feet, his long nightgown tucked into a pair of overalls. "I'll go tell Calvin and Grace," he said, and disappeared upstairs. In a trembling voice John Coolidge awakened his son to tell him he was President of the United States. The President dressed in a black suit, tie, and shoes, Mrs. Coolidge in white, and together they knelt by the bed and "asked God to bless the American people and give me power to serve them."

There were no photographers at the 2:47 a.m. swearing in.
This painting by a Boston Herald *artist, was done soon afterwards.* VDHP

It was a breathlessly hot night as the little group discussed what should be done. Mr. Coolidge at first wanted to wait until morning for the swearing in but was urged to do so immediately by Congressman Porter Dale, who with a group of men including newsman Joe Fountain, had come up from Ludlow. Could Colonel John administer the oath? Coolidge went over to the only telephone in the village at the store to call the Attorney General. The form of the oath and its legality established, a small group assembled in the sitting room of the homestead. Around 3 a.m. a temporary telephone had been set up in the kitchen, its line running in through an open window. However, the Colonel had no intention of keeping a telephone once the crisis was over.

Colonel John, who had dressed and shaved in cold water, now took his place on one side of a small marble table. On the other side, his back to the window, his wife on his left, stood Calvin Coolidge. Reading by the light of a single kerosene lamp, John Coolidge had his son repeat after him, "I, Calvin Coolidge, do solemnly swear that I will faithfully execute the office of the President of the United States…"

Then President Coolidge quietly said good night and went back upstairs to go to sleep. His father could not sleep again so easily but wandered about the darkened house till dawn.

Plymouth Notch would never again be the same sleepy little hamlet in the mountains. Next morning all the world knew of the dramatic scene in the homestead, and all the roads to the Notch were clogged with autos. The President came out to greet his neighbors, stopped to stand by his mother's grave for a few moments and then was driven to Rutland to take the train to Washington. The President said he'd prefer to take the Pullman but if they wanted to hitch a private car onto the down local he'd ride in it.

Herbert Luther Moore said, "For the next 24 hours things went wild in Plymouth…Ed Blanchard was driving his cows to pasture when a taxi came around and poked a cow out of the road. She got up and limped to the pasture wondering what had happened to the quiet little village…"

That evening neighbors noticed the poignant scene of Colonel John sitting all alone on the steps of his house. Later when questioned about his right to swear in his son, he said, "I didn't known I couldn't." About his opinion of Calvin's ability as President he answered with true Vermont caution, "I think he'll do fairly well. He did fairly well as Governor and I guess he'll do fairly well as President."

Colonel John poses at the sitting room table with the famous lamp. VHS

While almost everyone had been thrilled by the dramatic event, Aurora Pierce, the Colonel's housekeeper, was indignant when she read the newspaper accounts of the happening. She had missed it all, Mr. Coolidge deciding to let her sleep as she'd have to be up early in the morning to get breakfast. She didn't know when she tip-toed from her bedroom through the one next to it (the only way), that the man sleeping in the double bed had just been made President. What angered her was the report that the oath had been administered by the light of an "old spluttering, greasy" oil lamp. Housekeeper Pierce was ferociously neat and tidy. Her lamp chimneys were polished to perfection every morning after she scrubbed the kitchen floor making the breakfast eaters lift their feet as sudsy water flooded under the table. In her long stint as housekeeper at the homestead, Aurora managed to scrub Colonel John's painted kitchen floor so hard she wore it down to bare wood.

Aurora Pierce, aged 86, for forty years John Coolidge's housekeeper. JC

*Daily stage at Plymouth in front of the store, with John Coolidge.
Mail at the Post Office increased greatly in summer when the
President was there. Above the store was the modest Summer White House
Office where the affairs of the nation were transacted.* Both VDHP

Sharply contrasting with the simple Coolidge house, the gleaming Presidential Pierce Arrow limousine awaits its passengers. CCMF

Calvin Coolidge was President of the United States, but he didn't forget old friends back in Vermont. He and Mrs. Coolidge often invited them down to Washington knowing they'd enjoy a glimpse of the high places of the world. Mrs. Marion Hemenway, whose husband Rufus was a school mate of Calvin Coolidge, wrote her niece an account of a trip to Washington to stay at the White House in 1924. "When your aunt and uncle were a boy and girl together in Ludlow, Vermont, there was a little read-headed boy named Calvin Coolidge. They did not know that he was a Prince in disguise, but he must have been as now he is the most powerful ruler in the world."

Another young wife was a trifle disappointed in her trip to the White House. When the elegantly engraved invitation to stay with the President arrived in Vermont, she envisioned dinners of Lucullan splendor, swans carved in ice guarding imperial caviar, cakes of unimaginable delicacy. Being met by the President in the stately halls, her heart fell when he said, "Isn't it fine that you've come down from Vermont! Grace and I decided that since it's only four of us, we'll have a good old fashioned dinner of corned beef and cabbage."

It was during his presidency that his dry humor and poker-faced jokes became common currency, treasured as the essence of Vermont tartness. He understood that the quips helped with his image of the quiet man who wasted no time on fine words and who got things done, but the laconic speech hid the essential shyness of the man behind the impassive mask. It was not that he couldn't be positively verbose when the subject was one that interested him and when he was with trusted old friends. Much of the time he simply didn't feel like talking. He did his duty one day in Washington by planting a tree. He took a few jabs with the shovel, then fell silent. "Won't you say something, sir?" Mr. Coolidge peered into the hole for a moment. "Mighty fine fish worm down there." A Woodstock hostess found that the guest of honor on her right, Mr. Coolidge, was not exactly in a conversational mood until in desperation she hit upon the subject of clothes. The President perked up and asked, "Are you still wearing your winter underwear?" She said she wasn't, whereupon Mr. Coolidge said he was still wearing his. She managed to conceal her surprise at this confession that the President was wearing a union suit in the middle of summer. His chauffeur reported that his passenger said only one word on the long drive from Northampton to Plymouth. When a small furry animal scuttled across the road the President observed, "Woodchuck." He was often obliged to pose for his photograph and strangely enough didn't mind posing. "Let's talk to each other," he said to a dignitary, "it makes the picture look more interesting." But he was careful about handing out pictures of himself. When a visiting congressman called on the President at the Notch he asked for a new photograph of Mr. Coolidge saying that he already had one but it was when the President was Lieutenant Governor. "I don't see why you want another," said the President, "I'm still using the same face."

Although a shy man, the President enjoyed posing for the press. VHS

In the White House Garden. Calvin, Jr., center, died shortly afterwards. LOC

Calvin Coolidge, the careful, quiet Vermont Yankee, took his place as leader of the American people in the age of bath tub gin, of flappers and the Charleston, of raccoon coats and Stutz Bearcats. Millions of his fellow citizens withdrew their life savings from the bank for a giddy fling in the always rising stock market. It was the era of the Great Experiment, Prohibition, which paved the way for mobsters, hijackers and corrupted officials. It was the age of America on a grand spree. Amidst the glitter and the dazzle was the man who stood for all the Puritan virtues and who watched those traditions collapsing all about him. But as long as the bubble of prosperity floated, and it did for his five years and seven months in office, President Coolidge left well enough alone.

Calvin Coolidge won his own right to the Presidency in the election of 1924. In the summer of that year the Coolidge family had to endure the agony of young Calvin's death from blood poisoning. He was their second son and a promising attractive youth of sixteen. The President never really recovered from this last terrible blow. With his son's death went "The power and the glory of the Presidency."

Stoically he faced the presidential campaign. The outcome was never in doubt—the man from Plymouth had captured the American heart. However, his neighbors weren't going to leave anything to chance. They organized the Hometown Coolidge Club with its theme song of "Keep Cool With Coolidge," and in addition got together a dance band and eight dancers who set off on a five thousand mile campaigning jaunt across the country, ending in Bellingham, Washington.

"Keep Cool with Coolidge" was the theme of the touring old-time band. CCMF

*The President sets off for his second inauguration with
his wife and Senator Charles Curtis in 1925.* LOC

*Below, he entertains visitors on the lawn at Plymouth.
From the left: Harvey Firestone, the President, Henry Ford,
Thomas Edison, Russell Firestone, Mrs. Coolidge and Col. John.* VHS

That summer the Coolidges did a bit of entertaining while they were quietly staying with the Colonel. It occasioned one of the most famous of all the Coolidge pictures. One afternoon Henry Ford, Thomas Edison and Harvey Firestone dropped in at the homestead. Chairs were brought outside and the distinguished guests and Mrs. Coolidge and her father-in-law posed while the President inscribed the bottom of a sap bucket used by Calvin Galusha. He gave it to Mr. Ford saying, "My father had it, I had it and now you've got it."

His father's death was in the way of things, expected. Eighty years old, Colonel John had been in failing health during the summer of 1925 and the President had repeatedly urged the old gentleman to come down to Washington where he could be looked after by the President's doctor. Colonel John wished to die in his own house, but he allowed that Dr. Coupal could make a visit now and then to satisfy Calvin. Good Dr. Albert Cram from Bridgewater, however, would do for the long haul.

In January of 1926 the President had for the first time a direct telephone installed in the homestead so that he could speak every day to his father.

The end came for John Calvin Coolidge on March 18th, so suddenly that although Dr. Cram had wired on the 16th to the President the Colonel's death was near, he was still on his way when John Coolidge died.

A March snow storm with three feet of snow had virtually isolated Plymouth Notch from the world. Frantically men worked to get the road open from Ludlow to no avail. With axes, shovels and picks an army of workers managed to clear the road to Woodstock. The President arrived in White River Junction and transferred to the Woodstock Railroad, arriving at 6:30 a.m. In Woodstock plans had been well laid for the fourteen mile drive to the Notch. Six closed passenger autos equipped with new chains and manned by chauffeurs used to driving in winter were on hand. At Bridgewater Corners, after resting for a moment in a house that had a good fire burning, the party changed to sleighs which had been thoroughly inspected, supplied with hot bricks and drawn by strong, gentle horses. Every buffalo robe in Woodstock had been commandeered to cover the party. Turnouts had been shovelled and only doctors and midwives could interfere with the President's journey. Calvin Coolidge was too late. As the long procession pulled up to the village, the President saw that a path had already been shovelled to the church.

There is no doubt that young Calvin's death had much to do with his decision to retire from the Presidency and a third term with the famous announcement of 1927, "I do not choose to run." His wife had had no inkling of his thinking. "Isn't that just like the man! I had no idea!" Five years and seven months are enough he said. There were intimations that his health, never robust, had deteriorated during the Washington years. He had bouts of asthma and needed more and more rest, retiring at ten

The President's Vermont thriftiness was delightfully pictured in this 1929 drawing by Gluyas Williams, captioned "Crisis in Washington: Mr. Coolidge refuses point blank to vacate the White House until his other rubber is found." Permission of David G. Williams

*Back to the old two-family house in Northampton
but the sightseers soon made him move.* FL

every night and taking a two hour nap during the afternoon. He claimed
he longed for the quiet and private life of an ordinary citizen. Retirement
turned out to be more quiet and less private than he had bargained for.

The day he returned to Northampton from Washington he and Mrs.
Coolidge moved right back in their half of the two family house on Mas-
sasoit St. The only change was that the rent had gone up from $27 per
month when he was Governor to $36. But the tiny yard afforded him no
privacy. Slowly passing flivvers crammed with the curious forced him inside when he wanted to sit on the porch of an evening. Eventually he
was compelled to buy The Beeches, a comfortable estate where he could
walk and play with the Coolidge dogs, Tiny Tim, Mrs. Coolidge's chow,
and the President's white collie, Rob Roy.

The quiet boredom was more difficult to deal with. Mrs. Coolidge,
outgoing and friendly, enjoyed every moment of her return to small town
life and its many organizations. But for the man who had been at the center of the web of power it was a tremendous let-down to come back to a
law office but with no practice to keep him busy. He had decided against
taking up the practice again. He deliberately cut himself off from politics.
There was really very little for him to do. He did agree to write a daily col-
umn for a syndicate but that grew to be such a chore he didn't renew the
contract. Writing his autobiography gave him satisfaction and a good deal
of money. He was made a director of a life insurance company and presi-

At The Beeches. "I do not fit with these times." VHS

dent of the American Antiquarian Society and enjoyed the meetings of the Wednesday Club, an all male discussion group. Probably the happiest hours were those he spent in Plymouth over-seeing the building of six additional rooms on the homestead in the summer of 1932.

The boredom he managed to endure. What was a last and overwhelming blow was the stock market crash in 1929 and the criticism leveled at the Republican administrations. All his life he had preached that if you worked hard and saved your money you would succeed. Now for millions there was no work and the country's savings vanished in one bank failure after another.

At sixty he appeared to be an old man, tired and depressed. "I do not fit with these times," he complained.

On January 5, 1933, he came home early from his office, went upstairs to shave before lunch. Mrs. Coolidge came back from shopping, called for him but heard no answer. She found him lying on his back in his dressing room in his shirtsleeves. He had died instantly and painlessly of a heart attack. He was in his sixtieth year.

In the late afternoon of January 7, 1933, friends and neighbors of the thirtieth President of the United States gathered at the foot of Plymouth Notch cemetery. From a dull, pewter-hued sky cold rain turned to sleet. As the black umbrellas went up, all eyes were on an open grave dug that morning by Azro Johnson. The only spot of color in the somber gathering was a bright yellow horse blanket a father had wrapped around his little boy.

Speaking quietly to one another they waited patiently for the hearse and the family to arrive on the long journey from Northampton, Massachusetts.

At the morning's ceremony in Northampton, the retired President's home, the great ones of the country, the President, Supreme Court Justices and Congressmen had come to pay their last respects to Calvin Coolidge. Then they returned to Washington to take up their duties once more.

It had been a long, weary ride from Northampton to Plymouth. The 100-mile journey had been a slow one for at every crossroad small groups of people stood bareheaded waiting for the hearse and the accompanying cars to pass by.

At 4:30, as the last light faded from the January sky, the watchers by the grave saw the small cortege drive slowly up the steep hill from Plymouth Union. It was getting dark as the procession drew up at the cemetery. Six stalwart U.S. Marshalls carried the heavy bronze casket up the slope to the grave near the spot where the President's parents and youngest son were buried. A little group followed single file, Grace Coolidge with son John and Florence, his wife, and three old friends. There were no bands, no songs. Only the family and Calvin Coolidge's neighbors were there to bid him farewell. Someone held an umbrella over Grace Coolidge's head as a young bare-headed minister said the last simple words. Then, as the mourners turned to go, a bugle call rang out over the whitening hills. The villagers quietly walked home, leaving

The last light fades from the cold January sky over Plymouth Notch. EB

Calvin Coolidge among four generations of his ancestors. Next morning the clean snow had covered all evidence of the previous day's happening.

It was entirely fitting that Calvin Coolidge's final rites should be so simple and unostentatious. He lived his life in the same manner, even when serving as President of the United States. His handwritten last will and testament consisted of only seventy-five words, leaving everything to his wife. To the end, brought up in the stern ways of his ancestors, he remained a Vermont Yankee, born and bred.

It is also fitting that his most eloquent speech should have been about Vermont. It is one he made on September 21, 1928, at Bennington, Vermont.

In a letter, recently discovered at the Forbes Library in Northampton, Massachusetts, Grace Coolidge told how the President toured Vermont by train to see how his native state had coped with the devastating floods of 1927.

"The President had never liked to make speeches from the rear platform of a train," she wrote, but he had been greatly impressed by the still evident devastation and the progress made in recovery. "There was a large crowd at the station in Bennington, just such people as he had known when he was a boy. As he stood there on the rear platform one could not fail to feel an indescribable something of kinship, they were all Vermonters together. Suddenly, he began to speak. He had no notes. I cannot say whether or not he had been thinking that he might say something and so formulated it in his mind. However, I shall always believe that it was spontaneous, for he could do that sort of thing when moved deeply. I shall never forget the tone of his voice, as he spoke."

"Vermont," he said, "is a state I love.
I could not look upon the peaks of Ascutney,
Killington, Mansfield and Equinox
without being moved in a way that no other scene could move me.
It was here that I first saw the light of day;
here I received my bride;
here my dead lie,
pillowed on the loving breast of our everlasting hills
    "I love Vermont because of her hills and valleys,
her scenery and invigorating climate,
but most of all because of her indomitable people.
They are a race of pioneers
who have almost beggared themselves to serve others.
If the spirit of liberty should vanish in other parts of the union
and support of our institutions should languish,
it could all be replenished
from the generous store held by the people
of this brave little state of Vermont."

BIBLIOGRAPHY

Bryant, Blanche Brown, *Calvin Coolidge as I Knew Him*. Springfield, Vt., William L. Bryant Foundation, 1971.

———*Diaries of Pamela and Sally Brown 1832–1835; Hyde Leslie, 1887.* William L. Bryant Foundation, 1970.

Carpenter, Ernest, *The Boyhood Days of President Calvin Coolidge*, Rutland, Vt., Charles Tuttle Co., 1926.

Coolidge, Calvin, *The Autobiography of Calvin Coolidge*. New York, Cosmopolitan Book Corporation, 1929. Academy Books, 1972, 1984.

Coolidge, Grace, ed., *The Real Calvin Coolidge*. Plymouth, Vt., Calvin Coolidge Memorial Foundation, 1983.

Fuess, Claude M., *Calvin Coolidge, The Man from Vermont*. Boston, Little Brown and Co., 1940.

Lathem, Edward Connery, ed., *Meet Calvin Coolidge*. Brattleboro, Vt., Stephen Green Press, 1960.

———*Your Son, Calvin Coolidge*. Monteplier, Vt., The Vermont Historical Society, 1968.

McCoy, Donald R. Calvin Coolidge, *The Quiet President*. Boston, Little Brown and Co., 1967.

Ross, Ishbel, *Grace Coolidge and Her Era*. New York, Dodd Mead and Co., 1962.

Stillwell, Lewis D., *Migration from Vermont*. Montpelier, Vt., Vermont Historical Society Proceedings, Vol. 5, No. 5, June 1937.

Thompson, Sally, *Growing Up in Plymouth Notch Vermont, 1872–1895*. Plymouth, Vt. Calvin Coolidge Memorial Foundation, 1972.

Webb, Kenneth B., *From Plymouth Notch to President*. Woodstock, Vt., The Countryman Press, 1978.

White, William Allen, *A Puritan in Babylon*. New York, The Macmillian Co., 1938.

Wilson, Harold Fisher, *The Hill Country of Northern New England*. Montpelier, The Vermont Historical Society, 1947.

TRANSFORMATION

SPAWN

SPAWN®: TRANSFORMATION
ISBN 1 85286 834 1

Published by Titan Books Ltd
42 - 44 Dolben St
London SE1 0UP
In association with Image Comics™

This book collects issues 31 – 36 of the Image Comics' series *Spawn*.

British Library Cataloguing-In-Publication data. A catalogue record for this
book is available from the British Library.

First edition: June 1998
10 9 8 7 6 5 4 3 2 1

Printed in Italy.

TRANSFORMATION

SPAWN

TODD MCFARLANE
With GREG CAPULLO

TITAN BOOKS
in association with IMAGE COMICS™

Change is coming. He knows it.

The rhythmic clatter of train on track beats an uneasy counterpoint to the derailed pattern of Spawn's thoughts, signalling order where there is chaos, consistency where there is flux.

The city looms closer, he can feel its monolithic presence ahead of the goods train. The city, where he first awoke from a nightmare of pain to discover everything he once knew — about himself, about his life — had changed. Forever.

For a start, he was dead. Murdered and then resurrected five years on by the forces of darkness. He was no longer Al Simmons, soldier and patriot, he was Spawn, a general in the army of the damned.

His body had likewise been altered beyond all recognition. What once had been flesh now resembled putrescent meat. Where blood once coursed, necroplasmic energy now seethed. In place of cloth and hide, a living symbiotic costume with protective cape and chains.

But while the physical transformation was a wrenching shock to a mind already reeling from the trauma of a sudden, violent death and an equally deleterious rebirth, the worst was still to come. For something else had changed, something that turned his whole afterlife on its head.

Wanda had re-married. The beloved wife Al Simmons had sold his very soul to be with again was now wed to his former friend and colleague Terry Fitzgerald. And more, they have a child, a precious gift Simmons had never been able to grant Wanda.

Since then, as his own costume and abilities grew and evolved, and he learned more about his unwilling place in the escalating war between Hell and Heaven, there has been one constant in his fluid existence — conflict.

Around him the forces of light and darkness circled and gathered, anxious to exploit, manipulate or simply destroy this fledgling Hellspawn.

Spawn found himself hunted by the warrior-angel Angela and the elementally fired Anti-Spawn, both agents of Heaven, and every bit as remorseless and lacking in conscience as their demonic counterparts.

He was targeted by mob boss Tony Twist and his cyborg killing machine, Overt-Kill. Tormented by his former employer, the mercurial and lethal Jason Wynn. Accused and pursued by NYPD detectives Sam Burke and "Twitch" Williams.

Even among Spawn's own hellish kind there proved no respite from the ever spiralling cycle of violence and strife that surrounded him. Clown, a fellow demon with a predatory insectile alter-ego known as The Violator, sought and seeks still to discredit him in the eyes of *über*-demon Malebolgia, with whom Spawn struck his original infernal deal. In Clown's eyes, Spawn is an

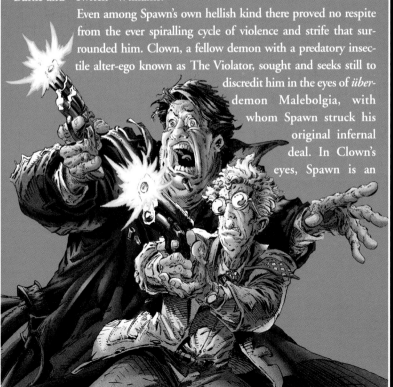

outsider, not worthy of such an exalted position in the hierarchy of Hell. Ostensibly sent to Earth by Malebolgia to guide and teach Spawn, Clown has his own curriculum... one that includes a short, sharp lesson in the art of extended manual dismemberment.

Spawn's only true ally, and indeed mentor, is Cogliostro, a mysterious old man who seems uncommonly familiar with the ways of the Hellspawn, and well versed in the lore of Hell. He, at least, understands the mutable nature of Spawn's existence, but is strangely reluctant to provide more than teasing hints and subtle prompts. He too knows that change is coming once more, and he fears it.

The goods train comes to a sudden, jarring halt, still some miles outside the city limits, shaking Spawn from his reverie. Huddled among dirty and unwashed bodies, Spawn feels strangely at home. It is not simply the proximity of the city, but the lost and disillusioned souls that surround him, fellow travellers on the last train to nowhere.

The only places Spawn feels at home are the city's alleys, the only company he keeps the down-and-outs who roam them. He has been absent from both for many weeks now, his trials manifold and exacting, and he yearns for the anonymous urban limbo and the precious illusion of peace it conjures.

Spawn wills the train to move, but it stubbornly defies him. He experiences a sudden, dislocating sensation of dread, a breathless pause filled with a thousand unanswered questions about what his future holds. Change. Change is coming, but what does that change herald? More conflict, more emotional strife? Is all that awaits him simply a new twist of the infernal knife that has already been thrust so deep in his soul?

Change is coming. But for better... or worse?

HE SITS ALONE. SWALLOWED WHOLE BY THE DARKNESS.

HIS ALLOTTED SPACE FAR EXCEEDS THAT OF THE OTHER, NAMELESS, OCCUPANTS.

TO THE MONOTONOUS RHYTHM OF WHEELS GLIDING OVER STEEL TRACKS, HE THINKS.

PLAYING THE SAME THOUGHT OVER.

AND OVER.

HER FEAR AND REJECTION, LIKE THE FLASHES OF LIGHT THAT SNEAK BETWEEN THE CRACKS, STAB AT HIM.

HE THINKS ABOUT IT AGAIN.

ANOTHER STAB.

HE SHOULDN'T HAVE BEEN SO QUICK TO ACT, HE TELLS HIMSELF.

BUT HE WAS MAD. EVERY-THING AROUND HAD BECOME A CHALLENGE.

HE KNOWS THAT ANSWER NOW: FEAR AND REJECTION.

SO HE BLINKS--A CUE TO CHANGE THE CHANNEL. THINK ABOUT SOMETHING ELSE.

HOME.

IT MUST BE NEAR. THE COSTUME TELLS HIM SO.

THE COSTUME-- ACTUALLY A SYMBIONT LIFE-FORM--HAS BEEN WITH HIM THROUGH A LOT. IT'S RARELY WRONG.

WHAT HARM IN FACING ANOTHER?

THE MECHANICAL HEARTBEAT BEGINS TO SLOW AS THE STEEL BEAST CREEPS INTO THE STATION.

HIS COSTUME GOES LIMP.

THIS IS SPAWN'S STOP.

THE TIME FOR BANDING TOGETHER NOW ENDED, EACH BEGINS WHAT HE HOPES WILL BE A NEW LIFE.

A NEW PATH.

ONE OCCUPANT CHOOSES A PATH NO OTHER CAN FOLLOW.

EVEN BEFORE IT'S STOPPED, A SEA OF HOMELESS HUMANITY SPEWS QUICKLY FROM THE BOX CAR. THEIR JOURNEY IS ALMOST OVER. THE PROMISED LAND IS BUT A FEW MILES AWAY.

THIS FEELS GOOD.

A CITY ONCE HATED HAS NOW BECOME HIS HAVEN.

'FILLED WITH AN ANXIETY HE DIDN'T EXPECT, SPAWN BREAKS INTO A SPRINT.

ADRENALIN PUMPS HARDER.

HE NEEDS HIS ALLEYS.

MORESO, HE *WANTS* THEM.

FINALLY ENGULFED IN THE BLACK BOSOM OF THE BECKONING SHADOWS, HE PAUSES.

THE FAMILIAR DARKNESS BLANKETS HIM WITH COMFORT.

THE KING HAS RETURNED.

C'MON, BOOTSY, GET A GRIP. FOR THE LAST THREE WEEKS YOU'VE DRAGGED ME HERE TO LOOK AT YOUR FRIGGIN' *FOOTWEAR*.

BUT I *MISS* THEM.

NOT FAR AWAY...

ORBITAL STATION ONE. THIS IS TERRAN HEADQUARTERS.

ACKNOWLEGED.

GENTLEMEN, LET THIS SERVE AS A FORMAL INTRODUCTION. I AM *RAFAEL*. I AM TAKING OVER FOR GABRIELLE, WHO HAS BEEN REMOVED AS COMMANDER OF TERRAN AFFAIRS.*

THE EMBARRASSING DEBACLE OF HER DEALING WITH THE CURRENT 'SPAWN'-- AND HER PERSONAL GRUDGE AGAINST A FELLOW ANGEL-- CREATED AN ATMOSPHERE WHICH SHALL NOT BE REPEATED DURING MY TENURE.

I WILL RUN THIS OFFICE WITH FAR GREATER EFFICIENCY THAN YOU MAY BE ACCUSTOMED TO-- AND WILL NOT TOLERATE FAILURE ON ANY LEVEL. DO I MAKE MYSELF CLEAR?

*AS PER *ANGELA* #3 --Tom.

AFFIRMATIVE.

GOOD.

GIVE ME A STATUS REPORT ON YOUR CURRENT TERRAN READINGS.

AT PRESENT WE HAVE THREE SIGNALS EMINATING FROM EARTH.

THREE! ARE YOU SURE?

WE'VE RECONFIRMED A NUMBER OF TIMES. THE READINGS ARE CORRECT.

TWO OF THE SIGNALS, THOUGH, ARE WEAK.

WHAT ARE WE TALKING ABOUT, THEN-- A *PARTIAL* DERIVATIVE? OR AN ENTIRELY NEW ENTITY?

ANALYSIS STILL INCONCLUSIVE... BUT ALL THREE READINGS OCCUR IN THE SAME FIVE-BLOCK RADIUS. THE AREA IS KNOWN LOCALLY AS "THE BOWERY," IN NEW YORK CITY.

YOU MEAN THEY'RE *ALL* IN MY *BACK YARD?*

IT *APPEARS SO.* THE TWO WEAKER SIGNALS ARE MOBILE SENTIENT BEINGS, INCIDENTALLY.

THIS IS *UNHEARD OF!* IT'S BEEN SPECULATED THAT A POWER TRANSFERENCE *MAY* BE POSSIBLE, BUT WE'VE *KNOWN* THE CHARACTER OF EACH SPAWN. *NONE* HAS EVER WILLINGLY RELEASED POWER TO ANOTHER.

THIS MAY PUT OUR PRIME TARGET IN A VULNERABLE POSITION.

HAVE YOU CHOSEN A NEW VESSEL?

AFFIRMATIVE. THIS SOLDIER WILL BE TAILORED TO OUR CURRENT DATA.

TESTS FOLLOWING OUR OTHER ATTEMPT INDICATE THAT THE ELEMENTAL FIRE *CONTENT* WAS ACCURATE, BUT INCOMPATIBLE WITH THE *SUBJECT.*

WE HAVE SINCE DECOMMISSIONED THAT FIRST SOLDIER. *

WE CONCLUDE THAT OUR NEXT SUBJECT MUST WILLINGLY EMBRACE THE VAST POWER OF THE FIRE.

Ah. A SOLDIER WITH A GOOD SOUL. *PERFECT!*

* JASON WYNN, IN ISSUE 16 -- Tom.

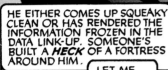

C'MON! NO! NOT AGAIN. THIS WON'T HELP ME FIND MY MURDER CONSPIRACY EVIDENCE.

ACCESS DENIED

HAVE TO GIVE JASON WYNN CREDIT-- HE SURE KNOWS HOW TO MAKE THE MOST OF HIS INFLUENCE.

HE EITHER COMES UP SQUEAKY CLEAN OR HAS RENDERED THE INFORMATION FROZEN IN THE DATA LINK-UP. SOMEONE'S BUILT A *HECK* OF A FORTRESS AROUND HIM.

LET ME TRY SOMETHING ELSE.

UNBELIEVABLE.

HIS ENTIRE FILE DIRECTORY HAS BEEN RECLASSIFIED. MY SECURITY CLEARANCE ISN'T ENOUGH TO EVEN GET *CLOSE* TO THIS SECURED DATA. THAT'S NEVER HAPPENED BEFORE.

THE BEST I CAN FIGURE, THOSE RECENT SECURITY CHANGES WERE DIRECTED BY AN OBSOLETE SECTOR. THEY WERE SHUT DOWN MONTHS AGO.

OLD JASON IS HIDING SOMETHING. I DOUBT EVEN THE PRESIDENT'S OFFICE COULD GET TO THOSE FILES.

MAYBE IF I REROUTE THROUGH INTERNATIONAL SECTOR F, CATEGORY 12...?

HE'S GOT THE WHOLE SYSTEM WORLDWIDE LOCKED UP!

GOD!

ONLY ONE OPTION LEFT-- UPGRADE MY STATUS... WHICH MEANS A TRANSFER INTO WYNN'S DEPARTMENT.

"IT HAD BEEN A MIRACLE," HIS MOTHER KEPT TELLING EVERYONE.

NO ONE, NOT EVEN HIS PARENTS, EXPECTED SUCH A LIFE CHANGE FROM **PHIL TIMPER.**

CONSTANTLY IN AND OUT OF JUVENILE DETENTION FROM EARLY ON. FINALLY CONVICTED AND INCARCERATED: TWO YEARS FOR FELONY GRAND THEFT.

IT WAS IN PRISON THAT PHIL GAVE HIMSELF COMPLETELY TO THE LORD'S BIDDING.

NOW HE'S THE MODEL CITIZEN, EVEN TRAINING TO BE A MINISTER AT THE LOCAL CHURCH.

AFTER ELEVEN SOLID YEARS SERVING THE LORD, HE STILL PRAYS EVERY NIGHT THAT HE WILL BE WORTHY OF GOD'S KINGDOM WHEN THE TIME COMES.

EARLIER TODAY IN NEW YORK CITY'S BOWERY, A "MYSTERIOUS LIGHT" WAS AT THE CENTER OF THE UNEXPLAINED DISAPPEARANCE OF ONE OF THE AREA'S LEADING CITIZENS. PHIL TIMPER HAD WORKED WITH THE HOMELESS THROUGH VARIOUS CHARITIES AND SHELTERS FOR ELEVEN YEARS, AND WAS HONORED LAST YEAR AS "VOLUNTEER OF THE YEAR" BY THE CITY'S MAYOR. NUMEROUS EYEWITNESSES TELL ESSENTIALLY THE SAME STORY, CNN HAS LEARNED. THEY CLAIM TIMPER WAS STRUCK BY WHAT APPEARED TO BE LIGHTNING, AND VANISHED. HIS GRATEFUL CLIENTS SCOURED THE AREA IN VAIN. TIMPER IS OFFICIALLY LISTED AS MISSING, BUT SOME HAVE EXPRESED DOUBT THAT HE COULD HAVE SURVIVED THE EXPERIENCE.

NEW YORK'S FINEST ARE STILL AT A LOSS TO EXPLAIN THE DISAPPEARANCE OF A PROMINENT GOOD SAMARITAN AT THAT BOWERY CHARITY MISSION EARLIER TODAY. A SOURCE AT THE POLICE COMMISSIONER'S OFFICE REVEALED THAT THE INVESTIGATION MAY INCLUDE THE CAPED VIGILANTE KNOWN AS SPAWN. THIS ELUSIVE MASKED FIGURE HAS BEEN A FIXTURE IN THE BOWERY SINCE HIS ARRIVAL SOME MONTHS AGO, AND HAS CONTRIBUTED MORE THAN HIS SHARE OF FUSS AND COMMOTION TO THE SCENE. OUR CRIMSON AVENGER'S RECENT EXTENDED, UNEXPLAINED ABSENCE HAS LEFT THE SHABBY LITTLE DISTRICT MUCH AS HE FOUND IT: DREARIER AND QUIETER THAN ANY RIGHT-THINKING PART OF MANHATTAN SHOULD EVER BE.

NOW, *BAM!* - OUT OF LEFT FIELD COMES ANOTHER NEW YORK MOMENT AS A MODEL CITIZEN *VANISHES* FROM THE MIDDLE OF A SOUP KITCHEN. THIS IS THE SAME WELL-SCRUBBED CITIZEN WHO WAS SHOWERED WITH GOLDEN HYPE DURING OUR PREVIOUS MAYOR'S FAILED REELECTION BID. COULD THE SORE LOSER HAVE CALLED IN ONE LAST FAVOR FROM ON HIGH AND HAD THE POOR LAD *SACRIFICED* ON THE ALTAR OF *UNWELCOME AMBITION?* THE BOYS IN BLUE, MEANWHILE, HAVE GIVEN THIS CASE THE SAME CARE AND ATTENTION THEY WOULD A STOLEN CAR RADIO IN TIMES SQUARE. JUST GOES TO SHOW HOW SINCERE OUR POLITICIANS ARE ABOUT THEIR COMMITTMENT TO THE LITTLE GUY. PICK OUT AN "AW-SHUCKS" SOCIAL WORKER, GIVE 'IM A TROPHY AT A PRESS CONFERENCE, THEN LET HIM GO ROT. GOD BLESS US, EVERY ONE!

AT 4:00 a.m., THE BOWERY'S BACKSTREETS FINALLY DRAG TO A HALT. EACH OF THE ALLEY'S OCCUPANTS HAS SOUGHT OUT HIS PLACE OF REST. A CAREFUL PECKING ORDER UNDERLIES THE COZY JUMBLE.

IT IS ONE OF THE SHORT PERIODS WHEN IT'S SAFE TO REST.

ESPECIALLY TONIGHT. WORD SPREAD QUICKLY OF THEIR KING'S RETURN. NOW THEY CAN SLEEP LIKE BABIES. AND LIKE A PROUD FATHER HE STANDS IN THE SHADOWS AND LOOKS DOWN ON THEM, HIS CHILDREN.

"THE MOMENT FEELS SO NATURAL," THE CREATURE CALLED SPAWN THINKS.

AS HE LISTENS TO THEIR MUFFLED BREATHING, A SUDDEN SENSATION GRIPS HIM.

HIS CHAINS PULL TOWARD SOME UNKNOWN DESTINATION.

"...Danger," THE COSTUME IS TELLING ITS HOST.

HE SPRINTS THREE CITY BLOCKS BEFORE ROUNDING THE LAST CORNER-- THEN STOPS DEAD IN HIS TRACKS.

HE CURSES THE TWISTED EXISTENCE THAT'S NOW HIS...

... AND CURSES THE FAMILIAR FIGURE BEFORE HIM.

WITH EVERY POSSIBLE OBJECT NOW SHREDDED, THE COSTUME AND ALLEY GO SILENT.

DEATHLY SILENT.

6:9:7:1

THE FIRST HINT OF LIFE COMES HOURS LATER.

NEW YORK CITY.

IN ANY LIGHT, THIS STRUCTURE IS A TESTAMENT IN STEEL AND GLASS. IT TAKES ON A MONOLITHIC MAGNIFICENCE AT NIGHT.

ITS CLEAN LINES ARE BROKEN WITH JUST THE BAREST OF ADORNMENTS, PLACED TO ACCENTUATE ITS *HEIGHT*. TO THE CASUAL ONLOOKER IT SEEMS TO TOUCH THE HEAVENS.

IN SOME INSTANCES, IT *DOES*.

AT THE MOMENT, THIS SELF-ASSURED FACADE HIDES A MASSIVE REORGANIZATION. THE *PREVIOUS* DIRECTOR OF TERRAN AFFAIRS WAS UNABLE TO DISTINGUISH BUSINESS FROM MISDIRECTED SELF-INTEREST. HER TAINT MUST BE SWEPT AWAY. SUPPLANTED.

THE BUSINESS OF BUSINESS, AFTER ALL, IS BUSINESS. THIS FRANCHISE WISHES THE COMPLETE CONFIDENCE OF ITS "FRONT OFFICE":

HEAVEN ITSELF.

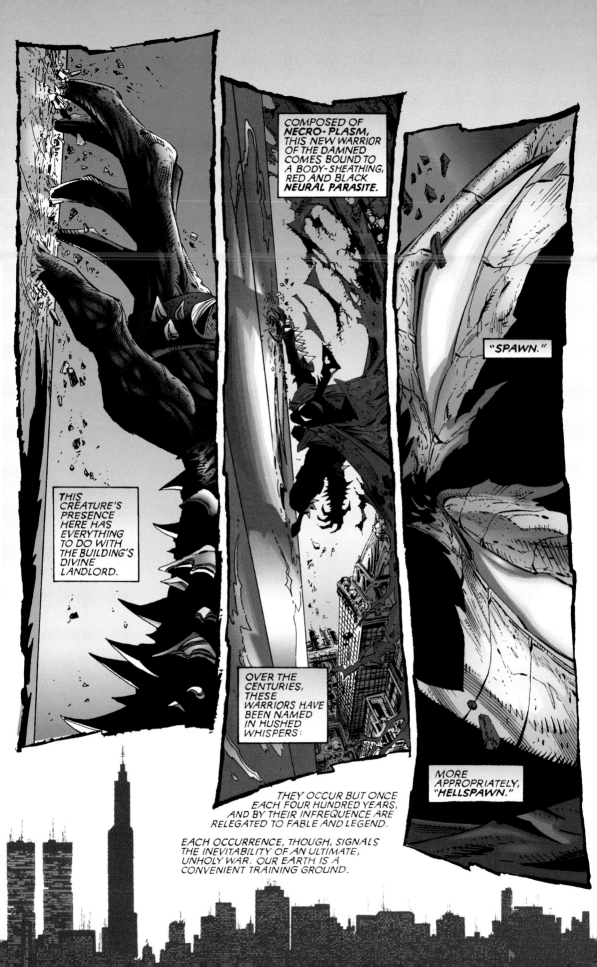

COMPOSED OF **NECRO-PLASM**, THIS NEW WARRIOR OF THE DAMNED COMES BOUND TO A BODY-SHEATHING, RED AND BLACK **NEURAL PARASITE**.

"SPAWN."

THIS CREATURE'S PRESENCE HERE HAS EVERYTHING TO DO WITH THE BUILDING'S DIVINE LANDLORD.

OVER THE CENTURIES, THESE WARRIORS HAVE BEEN NAMED IN HUSHED WHISPERS:

MORE APPROPRIATELY, "HELLSPAWN."

THEY OCCUR BUT ONCE EACH FOUR HUNDRED YEARS, AND BY THEIR INFREQUENCE ARE RELEGATED TO FABLE AND LEGEND.

EACH OCCURRENCE, THOUGH, SIGNALS THE INEVITABILITY OF AN ULTIMATE, UNHOLY WAR. OUR EARTH IS A CONVENIENT TRAINING GROUND.

THE PENTHOUSE SUITE OF OFFICES COMMANDS A VIEW WHICH SEEMS IMPOSSIBLY FAR-RANGING. WITH HER BACK TO IT ALL, THE NEWLY-APPOINTED DIRECTOR PREPARES FOR A MEETING. A VERY **IMPORTANT** MEETING. HAVING BEEN IN "THE SERVICE" NOW FOR WELL OVER **TWO MILLENNIA**, SHE UNDERSTANDS THE NEED FOR SUCH GET-TOGETHERS.

TODAY'S CONFERENCE IS TO FORMALLY SET THE **GROUND RULES**.

LIKE ANY SUCCESSFUL EMPLOYEE, **RAFAEL** KNOWS ONE'S **APPEARANCE** IS IMPORTANT AT THESE SESSIONS.

HER REPORTS ARE READY, AND THEY SHOW ALL CURRENT ACTIVITIES ARE **CLEAN**. A FEW NEW POLICIES OF HER OWN ARE ALREADY IN EFFECT, AND SHE HOPES **THEY** WILL APPROVE.

MS RAFAEL, THE **DIGNITARIES** ARE HERE.

SEND THEM IN, PLEASE.

UPPER MANAGEMENT'S BUSINESS PLAN MUST BE **FULLY** UNDERSTOOD... PARTICULARLY IN LIGHT OF **GABRIELLE'S** FIASCO.*

* SEEN IN THE *ANGELA* MINI-SERIES — Tom.

SHE'S FEELING **CONFIDENT**.

DOES THAT
INCLUDE THE
TORTURED
AND DAMNED?

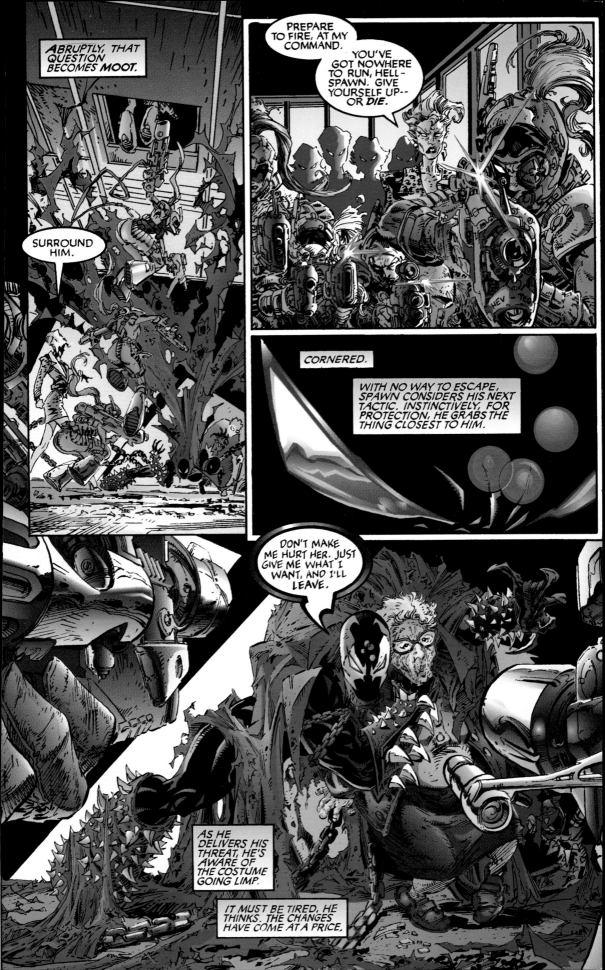

SPAWN'S MIND THEN FLASHES BACK TO EVENTS A FEW HOURS EARLIER.

THE REDEEMER HAD JUST TAKEN BOBBY, VANISHED RIGHT BEFORE HIS EYES. SPAWN WAS LEFT, POWERLESS, LYING IN STINKING DEBRIS IN THE ALLEY.

THEN IT HAPPENED. THE COSTUME AROSE FROM THE DEAD.

IT FELT DIFFERENT NOW. CHANGED SOMEHOW BY ITS OWN INTERNAL NEEDS. SPAWN SENSED ITS NEW MOOD.

IT WAS ANGRY.

THE ONLY THING LACKING WAS A DIRECTION FOR THE ANGER TO VENT.

I SEE YOU'RE STILL TRYING TO LEARN. YOU MIGHT NEED THIS.

CAGLIOSTRO. A MYSTERIOUS VAGRANT, WHO IN SOME STRANGE FASHION, KNEW WHAT SPAWN WAS GOING THROUGH.

YOU STILL HAVE MUCH TO ACCEPT. YOUR FRIEND NEEDS YOU. CONTROL YOUR RAGE SO THAT YOU MAY HELP HIM.

LOOK AGAIN.

WHAT IS IT?

INFORMATION.

BUT IT'S BLANK.

9 East 48th St.

AN ADDRESS. WHEN HE LOOKED UP, CAGLIOSTRO WAS GONE.

IT DIDN'T MATTER. SPAWN KNEW WHAT HAD TO BE DONE.

CALMLY, HE RECLINES IN HIS CHAIR. *JASON WYNN*, SUPREME DIRECTOR OF U.S. INTELLIGENCE AGENCIES, IS NOT GIVEN TO HYSTERICS.

I CAN'T TAKE IT ANY MORE! YOU HAVE TO **DO** SOMETHING! *ANYTHING!* THIS COULD RUIN OUR *CAREERS!* OUR LIVES!

CALM YOURSELF, MY FRIEND. NO ONE IS GOING TO DESTROY US.

ARE YOU *CRAZY?!* SOMEONE'S LINKED US TO *BILLY KINCAID!* HANGING OUT WITH A *CHILD KILLER* -- THAT DOESN'T GET *SWEPT AWAY* TOO EASILY!

HOW MANY *OTHERS* DO YOU THINK KNOW ABOUT THIS?!

I'VE RECEIVED A FILE CONTAINING CLASSIFIED INFOR MATION WHICH N OUTSIDER SHOULD HAVE. THE FILE WAS GIVEN BY SOMEONE CALLED *SPAWN.* *

*ISSUE 24 -- Tom.

WHAT!!

WHY WOULD SOME PSYCHO HERO HAVE IT IN FOR US?

ALL I KNOW IS, I'M NOT *ABOUT* TO LOSE EVERY- THING I'VE WORKED FOR. SO YOU *DO* SOMETHING ABOUT IT. *ANYTHING!*

BELIEVE ME, BANKS, I'VE ALREADY STARTED.

SPAWN BRACES HIMSELF FOR IMPACT. HE'D BEEN TOSSED AROUND BY THE REDEEMER AT THEIR PREVIOUS MEETING,* AND NOW DOUBTS, FOR THE FIRST TIME, WHETHER HE CAN SAVE HIS FRIEND.

HE'LL NEVER SETTLE THAT PROBLEM BECAUSE THE SITUATION HAS SUDDENLY CHANGED. IT IS ALIVE AGAIN.

THE COSTUME.

* LAST ISSUE --Tom.

ITS CHAINS, SWINGING WILDLY, SWAT THE ATTACKER IN MIDAIR. THEY THEN WRAP LIKE A COBRA AROUND THE DAZED REDEEMER.

IT IS ACTING COMPLETELY ON ITS OWN.

BOBBY! GET CLEAR OF IT-- HURRY!

THE REDEEMER REACTS LESS WITH ANGER THAN SHOCK AT THE SUDDEN **AMPUTATION.** UNCONTROLLABLY, THE STUMP SPEWS **ELEMENTAL FIRE,** DEMOLISHING EVERYTHING IN ITS PATH...

... ITS DEVASTATION THREATENING EVEN THOSE HE **SERVES**...

... YET **SPAWN** TURNS HIS BACK TO THE BARRAGE WITHOUT A SECOND THOUGHT.

GRANNY, I'M SORRY I HAD TO USE YOU EARLIER, BUT I DIDN'T HAVE A CHOICE.

I UNDERSTAND.

GREAT! NOW I NEED TO GET YOU OUT OF HERE. IT'S NOT SAFE.

AS HE TOUCHES HER ARM TO GUIDE HER, THE COSTUME BECOMES LIFELESS AGAIN. BEFORE SPAWN CAN EVEN REACT, THE REDEEMER **BLASTS** HIM, FACE ON.

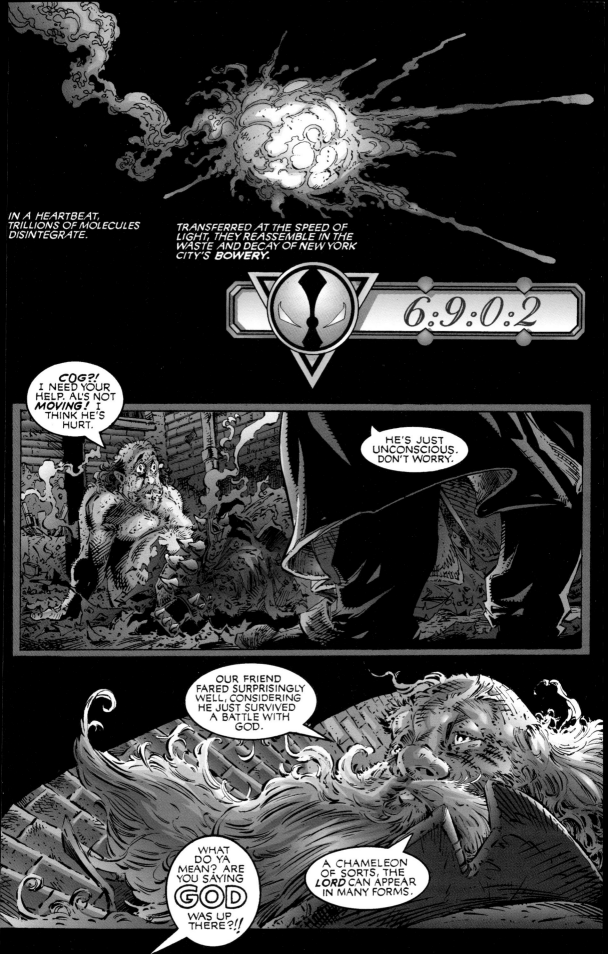

3

S H A D O W S

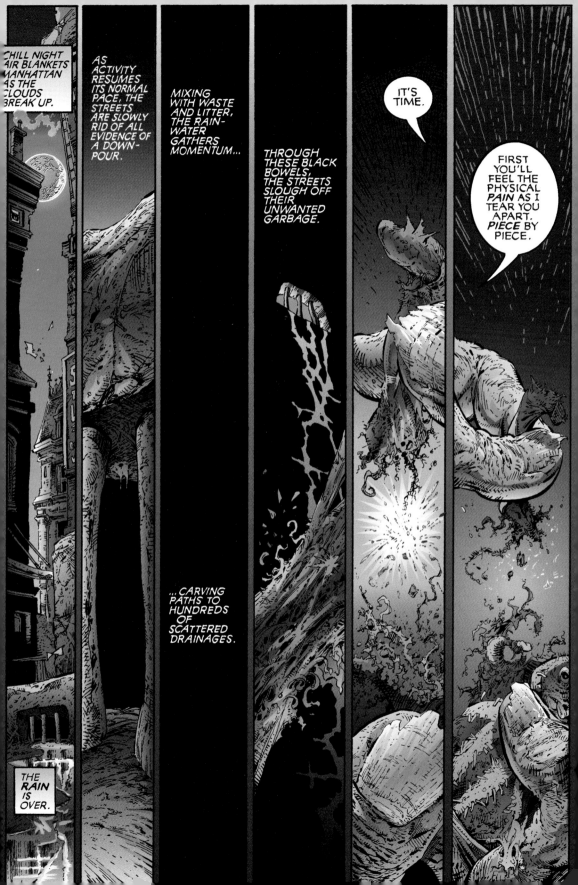

JASON WYNN, SUPREME DIRECTOR OF ALL U.S. INTELLIGENCE AGENCIES, PACES HIS OFFICE, BROODING OVER HIS CURRENT IMPASSE.

SOMEBODY DEEP IN THE ORGANIZATION IS TRYING TO SLIT MY THROAT. AND NOW I'VE GOT POLICE CHIEF *BANKS* CRACKING UNDER THE PRESSURE.

THAT *FILE*. HOW THE HELL DID SPAWN EVEN GET *NEAR* IT? THE GODDAMN SYSTEM SHOULD HAVE CREATED RED HERRINGS FOR HIM TO CHASE.

EXCUSE ME, SIR. I'VE CHECKED WITH PERSONNEL AND HIS TRANSFER IS COMPLETELY LEGITIMATE. EVERYTHING'S BY THE BOOK.

GET HIM.

WE *KNOW* FITZGERALD'S NOT SPAWN, BUT HE STILL HAS A STINK ABOUT HIM. THE WHOLE SET-UP IS FAR TOO CONVENIENT.

AH, MR. FITZGERALD, WHAT A WONDERFUL SURPRISE. I'VE LOOKED FORWARD TO THIS DAY FOR A LONG TIME.

THIS IS NO COINCIDENCE, BANKS. THE FILE. NOW *THIS*. AT LEAST IT'LL BE THAT MUCH EASIER TO KEEP HIM UNDER SURVEILLANCE.

HE'S BEEN BRIEFED AND BEGINS REPORTING TO YOU TOMORROW MORNING.

UNKNOWN TO WYNN, TERRY FITZGERALD IS PREPARING TO PLAY THE SAME GAME.

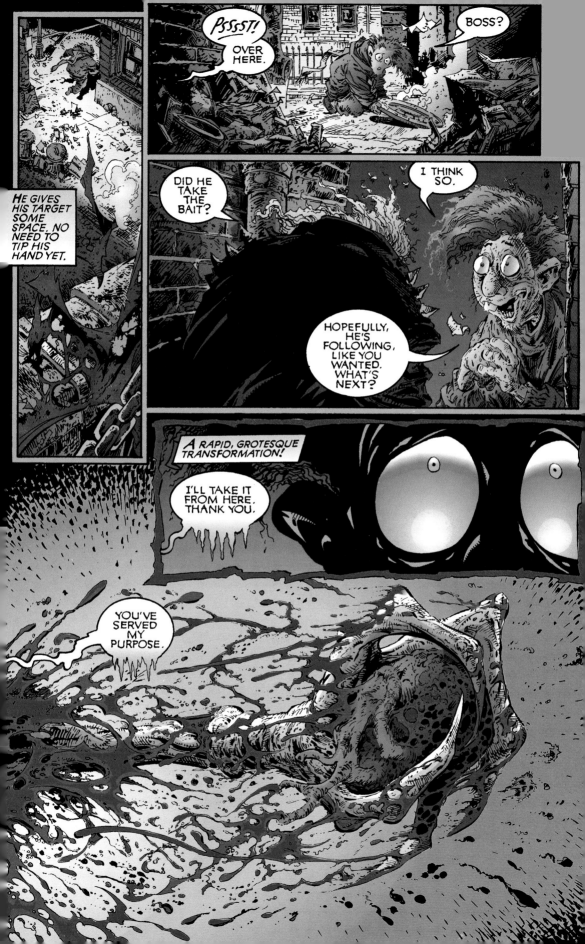

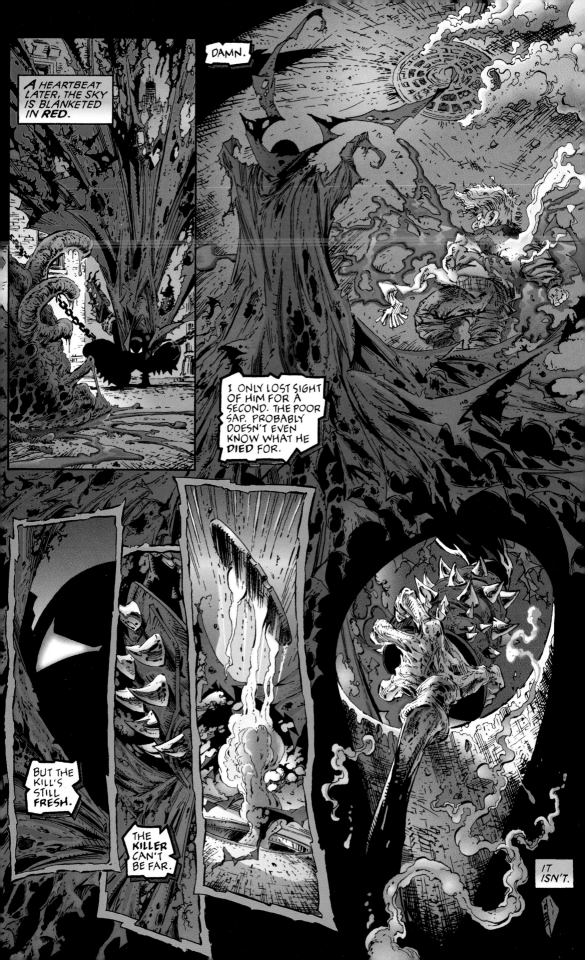

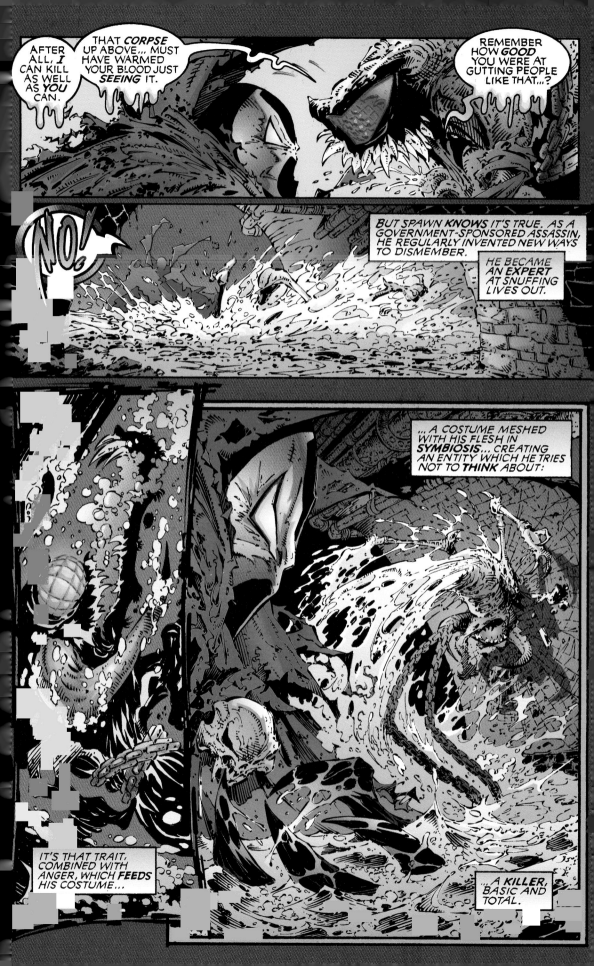

LIKE ANOTHER PIECE OF GARBAGE CAUGHT IN THE DELUGE, THE HERO IS SLAMMED FROM SIDE TO SIDE.

SURVIVAL IS HIS ONLY PRIORITY.

HE LEARNS THAT HIS BODY, NOW COMPOSED OF NECRO-PLASM, STILL NEEDS OXYGEN.

GASP!!!

AND WORSE. THE VIOLATOR HAS VANISHED. SPAWN EXPECTS, THOUGH, THAT HE'S SOME-WHERE IN THESE SEWERS-- UNHARMED...

... AND THAT HE'S AT THE MERCY OF THAT CREATURE'S NEXT MOVE.

6:8:8:7

TO BE CONTINUED...

4

THE CREATURE IS ROUGH. BRISTLY. **GHASTLY** TO THE TOUCH.

IT WAS BORN AN ETERNITY AGO IN THE FOULEST CORNER OF HELL'S EIGHTH LEVEL. ITS AVOWED PURPOSE, AS WITH ITS MISSHAPEN KIN, IS TO SERVE THE MASTER.

THE **MALEBOLGIA.**

DEEP IN ITS SHRIVELED HEART, IT KNOWS THE TRUTH: THAT THERE IS NO REASON FOR ITS EXISTENCE. IT DENIES THIS TRUTH, **DEFIES** IT... AND SO HAS CARVED ITSELF A **MISSION.**

THE CREATURE **FIGHTS** FOR THAT MISSION WITH A FIERCENESS AND LOYALTY RARELY SEEN AMONG ITS KIND.

EVENTUALLY THIS SERVITUDE LED IT INTO THE MASTER'S INNER CIRCLE.

IT WAS GIVEN THE FUNCTION OF 'SPAWN WARDEN,' OF INDOCTRINATING THE NEW OFFICERS IN HELL'S ARMY. THE DUTIES WERE SIMPLE.

BUT AS EACH SUCCEEDING SPAWN WENT OFF ON ASSIGNMENT, THE MONSTER'S PATIENCE CAME CLOSER TO ITS **LIMIT.**

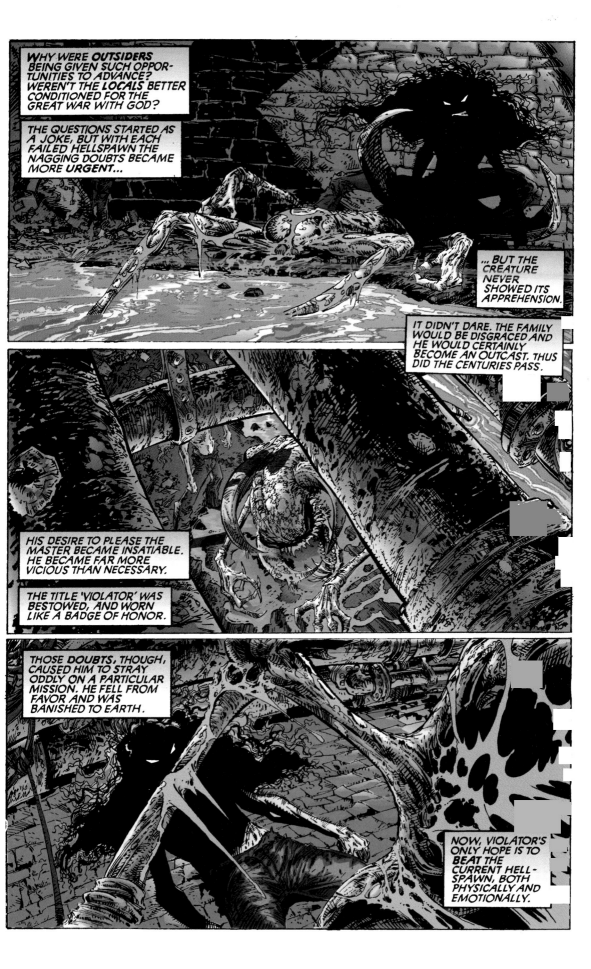

WHY WERE OUTSIDERS BEING GIVEN SUCH OPPORTUNITIES TO ADVANCE? WEREN'T THE LOCALS BETTER CONDITIONED FOR THE GREAT WAR WITH GOD?

THE QUESTIONS STARTED AS A JOKE, BUT WITH EACH FAILED HELLSPAWN THE NAGGING DOUBTS BECAME MORE URGENT...

...BUT THE CREATURE NEVER SHOWED ITS APPREHENSION.

IT DIDN'T DARE. THE FAMILY WOULD BE DISGRACED AND HE WOULD CERTAINLY BECOME AN OUTCAST. THUS DID THE CENTURIES PASS.

HIS DESIRE TO PLEASE THE MASTER BECAME INSATIABLE. HE BECAME FAR MORE VICIOUS THAN NECESSARY.

THE TITLE 'VIOLATOR' WAS BESTOWED, AND WORN LIKE A BADGE OF HONOR.

THOSE DOUBTS, THOUGH, CAUSED HIM TO STRAY ODDLY ON A PARTICULAR MISSION. HE FELL FROM FAVOR AND WAS BANISHED TO EARTH.

NOW, VIOLATOR'S ONLY HOPE IS TO BEAT THE CURRENT HELL-SPAWN, BOTH PHYSICALLY AND EMOTIONALLY.

AS ONE CHILD SETTLES INTO HER GRANDMA'S SWEET EMBRACE, ANOTHER AMBLES UNPROTECTED THROUGH AN URBAN CESSPOOL.

THESE STREETS HAVE, FOR ALL INTENTS AND PURPOSE, BECOME HIS HOME.

YO, TYRONE, WHAT IT IS.

IT'S THE MAN.

TUGGED AT. PULLED. THE YOUNG BOY BARELY PAYS ATTENTION.

AT TEN YEARS OF AGE THERE IS VERY LITTLE HE HASN'T SEEN.

HEY, BOY!

WHA...?

HE IS JUST ANOTHER OF SOCIETY'S FORGOTTEN VICTIMS.

I'VE BEEN WAITING FOR YOU.

FOR STINKY, THAT 'APPOINT-MENT' IS A SHORT WALK DOWN THE STREET, IN A BUILDING MARKED ONLY BY A SINGLE RED LIGHT DANGLING ABOVE A BLACK STEEL DOOR.

HE SHUFFLES PAST THE MAZE OF AISLES LITTERED WITH PORNOGRAPHIC MAGAZINES AND VIDEOS UNIMAGIN-ABLE TO MOST.

AT LAST, THROUGH A CURTAIN AND UNDERLIT HALL-WAY, HE ENTERS HIS PRIVATE CONFINES.

COME ON! COME ON!

OH YES. DO IT!

DO IT TO ME GOOD!

I PLAN TO.

THE NOISES CREATED BY THE WRESTLERS PURPOSELY MASK THE ACTIVITIES OF THOSE HIDDEN BE-HIND THESE WALLS.

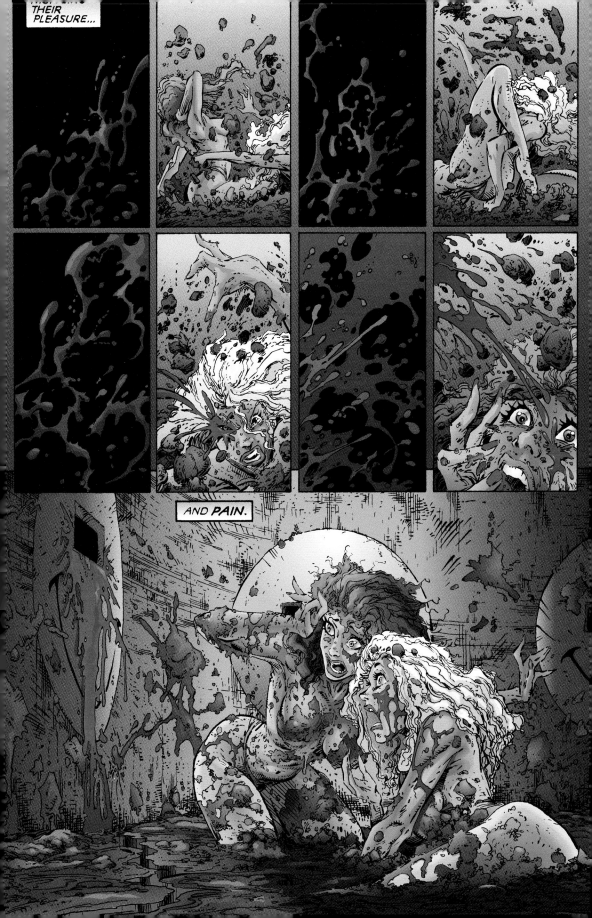

TWISTED IN BETWEEN PURGATORY AND LIMBO IS THE VAST WASTELAND OF HELL'S EIGHTH LEVEL. THE SHADOW OF THIS BLACK VOID CREEPS FAR CLOSER TO THE EARTHLY REALM THAN WE CARE TO THINK ABOUT.

IT'S HERE THAT THE ARMIES OF THE DAMNED ARE ASSEMBLED AND TRAINED, AWAITING THE SIGNAL TO BEGIN THE GLORIOUS WAR AGAINST THE HEAVENS: **ARMAGEDDON.**

THAT EVENTUAL WAR IS THE ONLY PURPOSE FOR THIS CREATURE, **THE MALEBOLGIA,** ONE OF THE HIGH-RANKING DEVILS. HE OVERSEES THE SWELLING SEA OF TROOPS, AND OCCASIONALLY CHOOSES OFFICERS TO LEAD THEM.

HIS LATEST HELLSPAWN-IN-TRAINING IS COMING ALONG AS PLANNED.

Delude yourself all you wish, Simmons, but you cannot run away from yourself.

There is a **reason** you were chosen from among the tortured millions.

Death. Evil. Blackness. Those seeds were planted in you at birth.

Soon. Very soon. All shall come to fruition.

THE SITUATION IN BOSNIA INTENSIFIES AS NEITHER BOSNIAN DIPLOMATS NOR THEIR SERBIAN COUNTER-PARTS SEEM WILLING TO RESUME PEACEKEEPING TALKS. THE PRESIDENT'S MUCH-PUBLICIZED VISIT TO BOSNIA WAS CUT UNEXPECTEDLY SHORT, THREE FEWER DAYS THAN PLANNED, AFTER THE BOSNIAN PRESIDENT WALKED OUT DURING OUR PRESIDENT'S PRESENTATION REGARDING THE ONGOING BORDER DISPUTE. CITING FAVORITISM TOWARD THE SERBS, THE BOSNIAN PRESIDENT ADVISED THE COMMITTEE THAT BOSNIAN PARTICIATION WOULD RESUME ONLY IF THE U. S. PRESIDENT WAS REMOVED FROM THE PEACE NEGOTIATIONS. CLOSER TO HOME, POLICE IN NEW YORK CITY ARE STILL INVESTIGATING A GRUESOME MURDER IN THE RED LIGHT DISTRICT. THERE ARE NO REPORTED SUSPECTS AT THIS TIME.

AS THE INTERMINABLE DRUG WAR IN NEW YORK CITY ESCALATES, ANOTHER PAWN FALLS, VICTIM TO A *GRUESOME* ATTACK IN A PORN THEATER. POLICE HAD TO RESORT TO DENTAL RECORDS IN AN ATTEMPT TO IDENTIFY THE BODY. SOURCES INDICATE THAT THE VICTIM HAD OVER A *DOZEN* BROKEN BONES. A BLOOD SPATTER EXPERT BEGINS HIS INVESTIGA-TION TODAY IN AN ATTEMPT TO DETERMINE WHAT, IF *ANY,* WEAPON WAS USED TO SEVER THE VICTIM'S HEAD. OFFICIALS ARE BAFFLED BY THE EXTENT OF THE MUTILATION, AND CANNOT DETERMINE IF THE ATTACK WAS COMMITTED BY A HUMAN OR SOME WILD ANIMAL. EVEN THOUGH THE RECENT *VAMPIRE* CASE HAS BEEN CLOSED, POLICE ARE NOT RULING OUT THE POSSIBILITY OF A CONNECTION. IS THIS JUST ANOTHER MEANINGLESS CRIME, OR A REVENGE HIT FOR A DRUG DEAL GONE BAD? BEFORE A MOTIVE CAN BE SUGGESTED, POLICE SAY THE VICTIM'S IDENTITY MUST FIRST BE DETERMINED. CREDIT WHERE IT'S DUE. SOUNDS FAIR TO ME.

BIG SURPRISE. OUR OVERWHELMINGLY ELECTED PRESIDENT HAS PUT HIS FOOT IN HIS MOUTH ONCE AGAIN, THIS TIME AS HIS PROPOSAL FOR ENDING THE BOSNIAN CONFLICT WENT OVER LIKE A LEAD BALLOON. THE PRESIDENT IS WASTING OUR VALU-ABLE TIME TRYING TO MAKE HIS MARK IN HISTORY. I GUESS HE'S NOT PLANNING ON RETURNING FOR ANOTHER FOUR YEARS, SO THIS WOULD BE A GOOD OPPORTUNITY. INSTEAD OF GETTING THE JOB DONE, AS *THIS* CITIZEN WOULD LIKE TO DO, HE PUSSY-FOOTS AROUND THE ISSUE, ACCOMPLISH-ING *NOTHING.* BACK AT HOME, WE KNOW HOW TO DEAL WITH SIMILAR PROBLEMS. FOR INSTANCE, LAST NIGHT'S GRUESOME MURDER IN NEW YORK. OBVIOUSLY THIS GUY, ANOTHER DRUG-PUSHING PUNK OR MAFIA THUG, GOT WHAT WAS *COMING* TO HIM. HE SCREWED SOMEONE OVER AND PAID THE PRICE. SHORT, SWEET, AND TO THE POINT. THE PRESIDENT COULD *LEARN* SOMETHING FROM THIS.

AT 2 A.M., INTELLI-GENCE DIRECTOR JASON WYNN HAD ASSUMED HE'D BE ABLE TO GET IN ANOTHER PRODUCTIVE ALL-NIGHTER.

MANIPULATION OF NATIONAL SECURITY MISSIONS IS BEST DONE FAR FROM THE LIGHT OF DAY.

Awww... DECEPTION AND DECEIT. GIVES ME A WARM, *SQUISHY* FEELING.

WHO DARES!

DOESN'T MATTER.

WHAT *DOES* IS THAT YOU'LL BE WORKING FOR *ME,* STARTING *TODAY.*

AND I'M HOPING IT'LL BE *PERMANENT.*

YOU SEE, I'VE DONE MY *HOMEWORK* ON YOU, JASON MY BOY. YOU'RE PERFECT FOR *MY* NEEDS AND WHETHER YOU KNOW IT OR *NOT,* WE HAVE A FEW COMMON ENEMIES.

SO, ARE YOU IN OR WHAT? THOUGH, COME TO *THINK* OF IT, YOU DON'T HAVE A *CHOICE.*

BUT THAT'S *YOUR* PROBLEM.

I DON'T KNOW HOW YOU GOT PAST SECURITY BUT YOU'VE JUST MADE A *FATAL* MISTAKE!

FORGET ABOUT THE PHONES. THEY'RE DEAD.

SPEAKING OF WHICH, YOU HAVE A THORN IN YOUR SIDE NAMED *SPAWN.*

COMBINE THAT WITH TERRY FITZ-GERALD. POLICE CHIEF BANKS. BILLY KINCAID. ET CETERA, ET CETERA, AND I THINK YOU GET MY *DRIFT.*

I'M LISTENING.

HIM AND HIS ADMINISTRATION ARE DUMBER THAN A SACK OF *HAMMERS.* THEY DON'T HAVE A *CLUE* ABOUT YOUR SECRET AGENDA.

LIKE THIS FILE... hmmm...

NAUGHTY, *NAUGHTY* LITTLE BOY. A FULL-SCALE *AIR SWEEP* OF A 'FRIENDLY' ARMY, ENGI-NEERED BY ONE OF AMERICA'S ENEMIES. IN RETURN, THEY GET A SECRET LINE OF CREDIT WITH A STRUGGLING *DEFENSE CON-TRACTOR.*

THEY GET TO CONTINUE THEIR WARS AGAINST YOUR ALLIES-- YOUR INTELLIGENCE AGENCY'S MORE ESSENTIAL THAN *EVER--*

--AND *YOU* COME OUT WITH TWELVE MILLION BUCKS OF LAUNDERED KICKBACKS IN YOUR SWISS ACCOUNT.

GET TO YOUR POINT.

TERRY FITZGERALD. I SEE BY THIS OTHER FILE THAT HE RECENTLY TRANS-FERRED TO YOUR OFFICE.

PERFECT. IT'LL MAKE THINGS EASIER. I WANT YOU TO *BEFRIEND* HIM. GAIN HIS *CONFI-DENCE...*

...WHILE AT THE SAME TIME DO A NUMBER ON THOSE HE *CARES* ABOUT. A SORT OF *JEKYLL-AND-HYDE* THING.

THAT MEANS HIS WIFE. KID. GRANNIE. WHO-EVER. PUSH THEM. *HARD!*

IT'LL DRIVE OLD SPAWNIE SIMPLY *BATTY!!* --WHICH IS A *GOOD* THING.

AND WHEN THE TIME IS RIGHT I'LL LET YOU *IN* ON SOME-THING.

LIKE WHO OUR HERO REALLY *IS.*

IT'S GOING TO GIVE YOU A HEART ATTACK.

PROMISE!

I KNOW. BUT IT'S STILL YOUR PROBLEM.

6:8:8:7

"BECAUSE, LIKE IT OR NOT, THERE IS A HOST OF OTHERS TANGLED IN YOUR WEB. IGNORING THEM WOULD WEAVE A LIFE WITHOUT PURPOSE.

"YOUR FRIENDS... LOVED ONES... WOULD FALL PREY TO MUCH EVIL."

AS THE DAY COMES TO A CLOSE, **TERRY FITZ-GERALD** FINDS HIMSELF ALONE AT HIS NEW OFFICE AT C.I.A. HEADQUARTERS.

FINALLY, HE HAS A CHANCE TO PURSUE HIS ONLY REASON FOR REQUESTING A TRANSFER TO JASON WYNN'S DEPARTMENT IN THE FIRST PLACE:

FINDING OUT WHAT HIS NEW DEPARTMENT HEAD IS REALLY UP TO.

THE GUY IS SLICK. RETRACING HIS TRACKS WON'T BE EASY, ESPECIALLY WITH ALL THE SECURITY CHECKS INVOLVED. BUT THERE HAS TO BE *SOME*THING HERE I CAN USE.

HIS INTERNATIONAL ACTIVITIES LOOK CLEAN, *ALMOST* TOO CLEAN.

THEN, A NOISE BEHIND HIM SNAPS TERRY BACK TO ATTENTION.

5

SET UP

Part One

SO I HAD A *LITTLE* INPUT.

FOR TWITCH, WHO HAD BEEN ANXIOUS TO RETURN TO WORK FOR DAYS, ANOTHER TWENTY MINUTES OF SOCIALIZING SEEMED AN ETERNITY. ONE CASE IN PARTICULAR WAS GNAWING AWAY AT HIM.

WITH A SUBTLE WINK TO BURKE, TWITCH LETS HIS PARTNER KNOW THAT IT'S TIME TO GET DOWN TO BUSINESS.

HOW LOVELY.

YOUR SINCERITY IS OVER*WHELMING.* A MAN GETS RIPPED *APART* * AND *THAT'S* ALL THE SYMPATHY YOU CAN MUSTER?

DO YOU HAVE SOMETHING ON THAT FEEBLE MIND OF YOURS THAT YOU'RE TRYING TO SAY?

NICE TO HAVE YOU BACK, LT. WILLIAMS. YOUR PRESENCE WAS GREATLY MISSED BY US ALL.

THANK YOU, CHIEF BANKS. I APPRECIATE THE KIND WORDS.

HE'S RIGHT, TWITCH. WE DID THIS OURSELVES. WE JUST WANTED YOU TO KNOW WE'RE BEHIND YOU, BUDDY.

* BLOODFEUD MINISERIES, #3 -- Tom.

I'VE *PLENTY* TO SAY... *SIR!*

THEN BE A *MAN* ABOUT IT, AND SAY IT TO MY *FACE.*

OH, I *WILL!* BELIEVE ME, I WILL. YOU'LL JUST HAVE TO BE A BIT MORE *PATIENT.* YOUR TIME IS COMING.

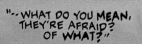

"-- WHAT DO YOU MEAN, THEY'RE AFRAID? OF WHAT?"

"YOU...

"YOUR POTENTIAL, TO BE EXACT.

"THE TRADITION OF THE SPAWN IS A VERY SORDID STORY, AL.

"EACH OF THE SPAWN CAME THROUGH THEIR BAPTISM OF FIRE WITH VARYING DEGREES OF SUCCESS.

"SOME FOUGHT THEIR NEW STATUS. SOME ACCEPTED IT, *TOO* WILLINGLY. BUT NONE WERE EVER ABLE TO *REVERSE* THE SITUATION.

"I GUARANTEE THEY'LL NOT LET *YOU* BE THE FIRST."

"YOU KNOW WHAT, COG, I DON'T GIVE A *CRAP* WHAT THEY HAD PLANNED FOR ME. *NO ONE'S* GOING TO DICTATE WHAT I DO

"UNFORTUNATELY, AL, THEY ALREADY *HAVE.* MEANWHILE, YOU'VE LEARNED HOW TO DEAL WITH THE *COST* OF USING YOUR POWERS...

"...HOW TO *KILL* MORE EFFICIENTLY...

THEN, EVERYTHING BECOMES BOTH HELLISH AND FAMILIAR AS SPAWN'S BRAIN IS SEARED BY A KALEIDOSCOPIC ARRAY OF IMAGES.

SCATTERED FRAGMENTS OF THE PAST FLASH HELTER-SKELTER. SOME THEN ARRANGE IN SHARP FOCUS.

THEY PIVOT AROUND THE HUMAN NIGHTMARE WHO WAS HIS BOSS. AL'S STRONG WILL COLLIDED WITH THAT OF HIS SUPERIOR... TOO OFTEN FOR EITHER OF THEM TO TOLERATE.

THE MAN, BLINDED BY HIS LUST FOR POWER, DEMANDED TO BE IN ULTIMATE CONTROL... THAT HIS WHIM DETERMINE THE FATE OF ALL SITUATIONS. ALL PARTICIPANTS.

HE GAVE THE ORDERS.

HE SANCTIONED THE KILLS, THE KILLERS...

HE CONTROLLED CHAPEL.

WHEN AL BECAME A BOTHER, HE WAS ELIMINATED. FOR THIS MAN, THIS DEVIL, ALWAYS HAD TO WIN.

WYNN! DA 1N YOU.

A HEARTBEAT LATER, THE IMAGES RETREAT. SPAWN IS UNSETTLED, BUT HIS NEURAL PARASITE COSTUME IS *INVIGORATED*. THE SYMBIOTIC LIVERY, THRIVING ON THE SENSORY INPUT, IS PUMPED AND READY FOR ITS NEXT CHALLENGE.

ITS HOST IS THOROUGHLY WIPED.

YOU OKAY?

FINE.

THEN IT'S TIME YOU BEGAN. YOUR MISSION SHOULD BE CLEAR.

JASON WYNN'S OFFICE, AT THE C.I.A. ...

AS I'VE BEEN SAYING, FITZGERALD, SECURITY HAS BEEN BREACHED RECENTLY.

I'D LIKE YOU TO HEAD UP THE REORGANIZATION OF OUR DATA SECURITY SYSTEMS. THE AGENCY MUST NOT BE COMPROMISED AGAIN, UNDERSTOOD?

YES, SIR.

LIKE A LONG SHADOW, WYNN'S PRESENCE CREEPS INTO THE LIVES OF TERRY AND HIS FAMILY.

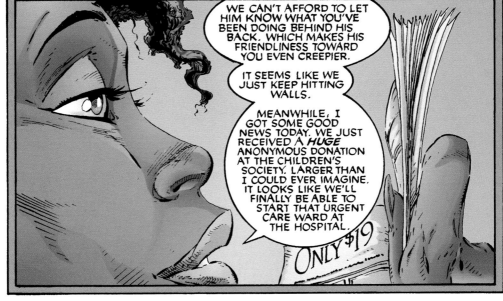

IT COULDN'T BE. NOT *THIS. NOT NOW.*

SINCE HIS RETURN FROM THE DEAD, NOTHING HAS MADE MUCH SENSE. HIS TWISTED NEW EXISTENCE HAS CONTINUED TO UNRAVEL *CHAOTICALLY,* EACH DAY BRINGING *NEW* PAIN.

THOUGH ONLY A SPLIT-SECOND OF TIME FLASHED BETWEEN HIS *DEATH* AND INITIATION AS AN AGENT OF *HELL, FIVE YEARS* HAD SLIPPED AWAY ON EARTH. SO, THIS CREATURE ONCE KNOWN AS *LT. COLONEL AL SIMMONS* WAS NOW DRIFTING EMOTIONALLY, LOST IN TIME.

HIS *WIFE*... REMARRIED... TO HIS *BEST FRIEND,* NO LESS. THEY HAVE A *CHILD*... SOMETHING *HE'D* BEEN INCAPABLE OF GIVING HER. *ALLIANCES* HAD CHANGED... AND HIS *IDENTITY* WAS NOW FOREVER *LOST,* EXCHANGED FOR AN UNHOLY *SHELL* OF *NECROPLASMIC GOO.*

HIS ONLY REFUGE HAS BEEN HIS PAST CAREER, THAT OF A COVERT *ASSASSIN* THE SERVICE OF U.S. INTELLIGENCE. RECENTLY-RECOVERED MEMORIES GA HIM THE FACE OF HIS *OWN* MURDERER. DECIDED THEN IT WAS TIME TO EXORCI A FEW *INTERNAL* DEMONS --

-- BY *KILLING* HIS FORMER BOSS--

--*JASON WYNN:* THE MAN WHO GAVE THE *ORDER.* THE MAN WHO, IN A BIZARRE TWIST OF FATE, HAD A HAND IN *CREATING* THIS NEW HELLSPAWN.

HE HAD HOPED TO MAKE WYNN DEATH EXCRUCIATINGLY *SLOW* REVENGE WAS ALL AL HAD LE HE HAD HOPED IT WOULD BRI A MOMENTARY RESPITE FROM THIS NIGHTMARE.

BUT NOW, INSTEAD, THINGS HAVE BECOME EVEN MORE *UNBEARABLE.*

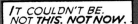

YOU TRAITOR

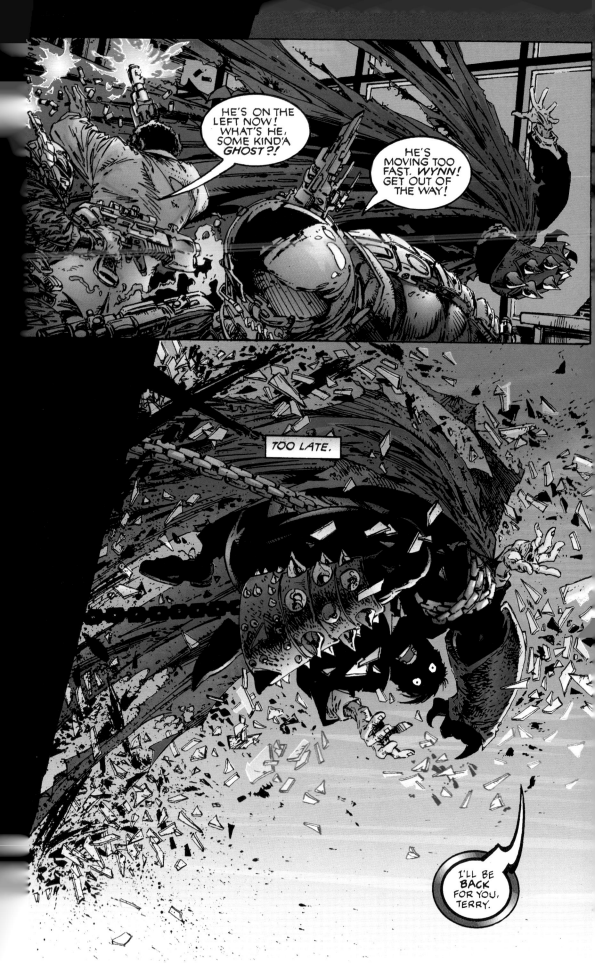

SOMEONE WHO GOT IN YOUR WAY.

WHO DIDN'T COUNT.

IN THERE! HURRY, PLEASE!

JUST STAY CALM.

DON'T MOVE! --BOTH OF YOU!

I'M JASON WYNN, SPECIAL SECURITY, SECTOR TWELVE. HE'S THE INTRUDER. GIVE ME YOUR GUN.

WHAT FOR?

I NEED A SACRIFICIAL PIG.

A BEAT LATER... OUTSIDE THE OFFICE...

HELP! THE CREATURE'S GONE MAD! HE'S KILLED THE GUARD!

"--SHRED HIM!"

CONTACT POINT. THIS IS COMMANDER COOPER OF THE U.S. ARMY. WE'VE SPOTTED YOUR TARGET. WHAT ARE YOUR ORDERS?

"TERMINATE ON SIGHT."

AFFIRMATIVE. 10-4.

CHOPPER TWO, DEPLOY TRACKING MISSILES. WE'LL CORNER THE TARGET TO THE EAST, THEN FALL OUT.

YOU FOLLOW BEHIND FOR THE CLEAR SHOT.

I APPLAUD YOU ON YOUR EFFORTS TO BANISH ME, BUT BY NOW YOU'VE BECOME PAINFULLY AWARE HOW *USELESS* THAT WAS. YOU *SEE*, BOY, THERE'S A NATURAL PECKING ORDER IN LIFE. *SOME* OF US ARE MEANT FOR *GRANDEUR* WHILE OTHERS, LIKE *YOURSELF*, FLAIL TRAGICALLY THROUGH LIFE, AMOUNTING TO *NOTHING*.

OR, TO PUT IT MORE CLEARLY, YOU'RE OUT OF YOUR LEAGUE WITH YOUR *NECK* STUCK OUT AND NOW. IT'S ABOUT TO GET *CHOPPED*.

YOU'VE BEEN A PAIN TO ME FOR OVER FOUR YEARS-- BUT *NO MORE!*

PUL-*EASSE!* CAN YOU BE A BIT *MORE* MELODRAMATIC.

DAMN IT, BURKE! THIS ISN'T A *JOKE* ANY LONGER. THOUGH I'D *DEARLY* LOVE TO *FIRE* YOUR ASS RIGHT NOW, THAT WOULD RAISE SOME EYE-BROWS. ESPECIALLY *NOW*. NO... I'M A *PATIENT* MAN. I'LL PUT UP WITH YOU TWO FOR THE TIME BEING.

BUT I SWEAR IF *EITHER* OF YOU EVEN *SNEEZES* WRONG I'LL MAKE SURE YOU LOSE EVERYTHING. YOUR JOBS. YOUR PENSIONS. YOU *NAME* IT.

IN THE MEANTIME I SUGGEST YOU LOOK FOR ANOTHER LINE OF WORK BECAUSE AS SOON AS THE HEAT DIES DOWN AROUND HERE YOU'RE *DONE*.

AND ONCE YOU'RE ON YOUR OWN, IF I WERE YOU, I'D CHECK OVER MY SHOULDER REGULARLY, BECAUSE I'M NOT ABOUT TO FORGET WHAT YOU TRIED TO *DO* TO ME!

UM, EXCUSE ME...

SCREW YOU!

YOU DON'T THREATEN ME *OR* MY FRIEND, UNDER*STAND?* YOU WANT TO FIGHT US THEN BE MY GUEST-- 'CAUSE YOU KNOW WHAT? I'M NOT AFRAID OF *YOUR* KIND.

SEE, I'VE KEPT A *COPY* OF YOUR FILE AS A BACK-UP, AND IF *ANYTHING* HAPPENS TO ME OR SAM, I'VE ARRANGED FOR IT TO HIT *EVERY* MAJOR NEWS-PAPER AND TALK SHOW IN THIS COUNTRY. AND *BELIEVE* ME-- I *DON'T BLUFF*.

AS FOR YOUR PATHETIC ATTEMPTS TO *INTIMIDATE* US, LET ME REFRESH YOUR MEMORY ON ONE LITTLE MATTER. I'M A *SHARPSHOOTER*-- BEST IN THE *CITY*. YOU WANT A BULLET DEAD CENTER THROUGH EACH EYE, THEN *PUSH* ME.

GO GET 'IM, TWITCH.

BECAUSE I MADE A PLEDGE YEARS AGO TO RID SOCIETY OF SCUM LIKE *YOU*.

WE NOW SHIFT TO THE SUBURBS-- *QUEENS*-- A SHORT TIME LATER...

WELL *THANK* YOU, WANDA, FOR SUCH A *BEAUTIFUL* DAY. THE FRESH *AIR* SURE FELT GOOD. THOUGH I'M SORRY I COULDN'T WALK THE PARK QUITE AS FAST AS *YOU* TWO.

AN AFTERNOON AWAY FROM THE HOUSE IS A PLEASURE I DON'T *GET* TOO OFTEN. BUT I DO EN*JOOY--!*

--*URK!--*

CYAN! PLEASE! NOT SO HARD. YOU HAVE TO BE GENTLE WHEN YOU GIVE GREAT-GRANNIE A HUG.

GRACIOUS! I *DO* LOVE THIS CHILD OF YOURS, WANDA. ALWAYS MAKING ME FEEL SO GOOD.

MMM!

WELL, SHE JUST GETS SO *EXCITED* ABOUT COMING OVER HERE. ISN'T THAT RIGHT, SWEETY.

I APPRECIATE YOU SPENDING A BIT MORE TIME. TOO BAD TERRY COULDN'T MAKE IT.

GRAMMA.

YEAH. HE MUST BE WORKING LATE TONIGHT. YOU KNOW, TRYING TO IMPRESS THE NEW BOSS. HOPEFULLY, HE'LL COME NEXT VISIT.

THAT'D BE NICE. I MISS HIS COMPANY, TOO. BUT I KNOW HOW *BUSY* YOU BOTH ARE.

I WISH IT WASN'T TRUE. BETWEEN MY CHARITY WORK AND SOME NEW CLASSES, I CAN'T REMEMBER THE LAST TIME TERRY AND I JUST SAT DOWN AND TURNED ON THE TV.

...CONTINUE OUR LIVE COVERAGE OF TONIGHT'S BOMBING AT NEW YORK CITY'S MERRILL-LYNCH BUILDING, AND THE REPORTED ASSAULT ON THE C.I.A HEADQUARTERS NEXT DOOR. POLICE SOURCES ARE CAUTIOUSLY OPTIMISTIC THAT NO ONE DIED IN THIS ATTACK ON THE NATION'S LARGEST BROKERAGE INSTITUTION. THE UPPER TWO STORIES OF THIS BUILDING, WHICH HOUSE THE GYM AND CAFETERIA, HAD ALREADY BEEN SECURED FOR THE NIGHT. IT IS BELIEVED THAT NO EMPLOYEES WERE WORKING LATE IN ANY OTHER AREAS, AND MOST HAVE BEEN LOCATED AT THEIR HOMES. THE WHITE HOUSE DE-NIES REPORTS THAT AN AS-YET UNIDEN-TIFIED TERRORIST GROUP HAD STAGED THE EVENT AS A REJECTION OF THE ADMINSTRATION'S PEACE NEGOTIA-TIONS IN THE MIDDLE EAST.

OFF THE RECORD SPECULATION FROM *MY* ANONYMOUS SOURCES IS THAT A *HOME-GROWN* TERRORIST GROUP WAS BLOWING A LOUD RASPBERY AT THE PRESIDENT'S MIDDLE EAST PEACE EFFORT. AT THE SAME TIME, FRENZIED SPIN DOCTORS ARE QUICK TO DISPEL ANY *HINT* OF A CONNECTION TO THE OKLAHOMA CITY INCIDENT. *"JUST THE ACTIONS OF ANOTHER DERANGED INDI-VIDUAL"*, THEY TELL US, WHICH IS TO SAY, NOBODY HAS A *CLUE.* CONFUS-ING MATTERS EVEN FURTHER IS THE RAPID INVOLVEMENT OF OUR NATION'S MILITARY FORCES. SOME EYE-WITNESSES SAY IT WAS THE *PRESENCE* OF THE HELICOPTERS THAT TRIGGERED THE BOMBINGS, WHILE OTHERS MAIN-TAIN THE DAMAGE WAS DONE *BEFORE* THEIR ARRIVAL. IN EITHER CASE, EVERY AGENCY IN THE CITY IS NOW ON ALERT FOR POSSIBLE FOLLOW-UP ACTION. MEANWHILE, ALL EYES TURN TO THE WHITE HOUSE FOR SOMEONE -- *ANY-ONE* -- TO EXPLAIN IT ALL FOR US.

ARE YOU *KIDDING* ME?! THIS ISN'T A CASE OF WHACKED-OUT IDIOTS LOOKING FOR ATTENTION, *NO* SIR! WHAT WE'RE LOOK-ING AT IS *RETALIATION.* SOME GROUP IS SENDING A MESSAGE TO THOSE WHO HIDE IN THE SHADOWS, PLAYING DOPEY SPY GAMES WITH OUR TAX DOLLARS. NO ONE IS ADMITTING ANYTHING, BUT ANY-ONE WHO THINKS THE C.I.A. ATTACK AND THE MERRILL-LYNCH BOMBING ARE UNRELATED IS EITHER *IGNORANT* OR *STUPID.* THIS WHOLE *THING* SMELLS ROTTEN. WORSE THAN THAT, THE PRESI-DENT AND HIS AIDES ARE STONEWALLING. DIDN'T WE ELECT THESE GUYS BECAUSE THE *PREVIOUS* BUNCH WERE CLAIMING "DENIABILITY" TOO OFTEN?! SO NOW WE HAVE THE *ARMY*, THE *FINANCIAL* COM-MUNITY AND THE *CENTRAL INTELLI-GENCE* BOYS RUNNING AROUND IN AN ANT FARM, BUT FOR A CHANGE WE'VE GOT A MAGNIFYING GLASS ON 'EM. I GUARANTEE THAT *SOME*ONE'S HIDING SOMETHING, AND THIS TIME WE JUST MIGHT FIND OUT WHAT IT IS.

FINALLY ALONE, IT TAKES ALMOST TWO HOURS FOR WYNN TO FALL ASLEEP. HIS MIND'S RESISTANCE SUCCUMBS GRUDGINGLY TO HIS BODY'S DEMANDS.

MY MY. DON'T WE LOOK LIKE A LITTLE ANGEL, LYING THERE.

WHAT?

HEY, STUD! REMEMBER *ME?* 'COURSE YOU DO. ANYWAYS, IT SEEMS LIKE YOU'VE GOTTEN YOURSELF INTO A BIT OF A TIGHT *SQUEEZE.*

AGAIN.

WELL... YOU'RE LUCKY I'VE TAKEN A *SHINE* TO YOU. SEE, OUT OF THE GOODNESS OF MY BLACK HEART I'M GOING TO DO YOU ANOTHER HUGE *FAVOR.* REMEMBER SPAWN'S ATTACK ON YOUR OFFICE? WELL, IT'LL APPEAR *EXACTLY* LIKE THE WORK OF A TERRORIST FROM ABROAD-- ANOTHER TRADE CENTER BOMBING, IF YOU WILL. NO ONE WILL BE THE WISER.

I KNOW! I KNOW! YOU WANT TO KISS ME. WELL, LET'S NOT SPOIL THE *MOMENT.*

OH -- AND I SHOULD MENTION, IN ALL HONESTY, THAT YOU'VE BEEN DOING A DECENT JOB OF PUSHING SPAWN'S BUTTONS. DRIVING HIM INSANE, THAT'S *GREAT!*

BUT PUSH TOO HARD AND HE'LL KILL YOU IN A HEARTBEAT. WE CAN'T HAVE THAT. YOU'RE TOO IMPORTANT.

Y'KNOW, I'VE SEEN *HELL'S* DOSSIER ON YOU. PURE EVIL'S A RARE COMMODITY AMONG YOU HUMANS -- AND PAL, YOU ARE *WAY* OFF THE CHARTS. WE NEED YOU *INTACT.*

SO *PUSH* SPAWN. BUT TRY AND KEEP SOME *DISTANCE.*

EVENING, MR. WYNN. TIME FOR YOUR MEDICINE. HOPE YOU'VE BEEN GETTING SOME REST.

I'M TRYING.

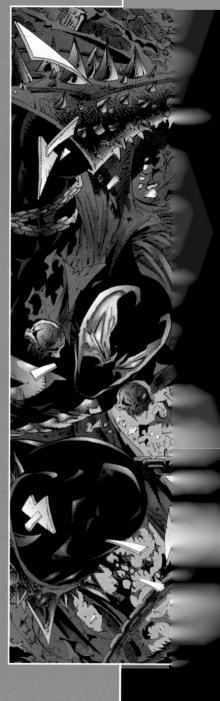

THE HOMECOMING"

Todd McFarlane – *story*
Todd McFarlane and Greg Capullo – *art*
Tom Orzechowski – *letters & copy editor*
Steve Oliff and Olyoptics – *colour*

APPEARANCES"

Todd McFarlane – *story*
Todd McFarlane and Greg Capullo – *art*
Tom Orzechowski – *letters & copy editor*
Steve Oliff and Olyoptics – *colour*

SHADOWS"

Todd McFarlane – *story*
Todd McFarlane and Greg Capullo – *art*
Tom Orzechowski – *letters & copy editor*
Steve Oliff and Olyoptics – *colour*

RIPPLES"

Todd McFarlane – *story*
Todd McFarlane and Greg Capullo – *art*
Tom Orzechowski – *letters & copy editor*
Steve Oliff, Quinn Supplee and Olyoptics – *colour*

SET UP" PART ONE

Todd McFarlane – *story & inks*
Greg Capullo – *pencils*
Tom Orzechowski – *letters & copy editor*
Steve Oliff, Quinn Suppleeand Olyoptics – *colour*

SET UP" PART TWO

Todd McFarlane – *story & inks*
Greg Capullo – *pencils*
Tom Orzechowski – *letters & copy editor*
Steve Oliff, Quinn Suppleeand Olyoptics – *colour*

Special thank-you to Kevin Conrad, Chance Wolf & Julia Simmons

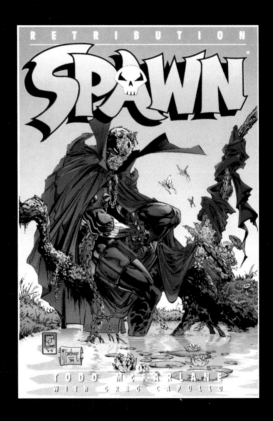